IESE CITIES IN MOTION:
INTERNATIONAL URBAN BEST PRACTICES

CITIES AND INTERNATIONAL OUTREACH:
THE ERA OF THE GLOBAL CITY

VOLUME 5

PROF. PASCUAL BERRONE
PROF. JOAN ENRIC RICART COSTA
ANA ISABEL DUCH T-FIGUERAS

IESE
Business School
University of Navarra

Copyright © 2019 Pascual Berrone, Joan Enric Ricart Costa, Ana Isabel Duch T-Figueras

All rights reserved.

ISBN-13: 978-1695103290

ISBN-10: 1695103290

We gratefully acknowledge the financial support of the Agencia Estatal de Investigación (AEI) of the Ministry of Economy and Competitiveness—ECO2016-79894-R (MINECO/FEDER), the Schneider-Electric Sustainability and Business Strategy Chair, the Carl Schroeder Chair in Strategic Management and the IESE's High Impact Projects initiative (2017/2018).

Preface to the Book Series

"IESE CITIES IN MOTION:
International Urban Best Practices"

The world is experiencing the largest increase in urban growth in history. Today, more than half of the world's population lives in cities and it is forecast that the percentage of urban residents in the global population will increase to almost 70% by 2050. This unprecedented growth in urbanization has the potential to bring significant benefits for citizens, such as new jobs and well-being, along with overall economic growth. However, rapid urbanization also multiplies the number, size and complexity of the challenges faced by cities, such as increasing pressure on scarce resources, greater demand for basic infrastructure and public services, as well as greater socioeconomic inequality.

Cities must be able to solve economic, social and environmental problems simultaneously, in all cases with the aim of improving the welfare and quality of life of their residents. In their search for sustainable, equitable, connected and innovative city models, municipal leaders around the world look at the experiences of other cities to get ideas and study best practices. Although there is no "one size fits all" solution, this book series aims to help city managers in their endeavors to create urban areas that are environmentally, economically and socially sustainable. With this objective, this series will examine some of the actions, projects and initiatives that have had the best results in cities internationally, so that other cities around the world can build on the most successful approaches and adapt them to their local realities and needs.

The book series is based on the IESE Cities in Motion model, which includes an innovative approach to the governance of cities and a new urban model for the 21st century based on 10 key areas or dimensions: human capital, social cohesion, the economy, public management, governance, mobility and transportation, the environment, urban planning, technology and international outreach. Each volume in this series provides an overview of the main challenges regarding a specific dimension and describes some of the most successful initiatives and actions that have been adopted regarding that area in different cities around the world. Despite the fact that each area is covered in a separate volume of its own, all the key areas must be seen as different parts of a system that works as one. All the dimensions are interconnected and actions in one area affect other areas at the same time. Therefore, the available resources must be shared and managed together in order to achieve sustainable, lively, healthy and safe cities.

With this book series, we aim to contribute to the debate on smart urban governance by developing valuable ideas and innovative tools that can lead to smarter and more sustainable cities, while promoting real change at the local level and improving people's quality of life. We believe that current urban challenges are not only problems to be solved, but opportunities to be exploited.

Prior volumes of this series:

Vol. 1: *Cities and the Environment: The challenge of becoming green and sustainable,* CreateSpace, 2016.

See, **"Greening Up in the City"**. Available at: https://www.amazon.com/dp/1523965789.

"Responsible for the vast majority of the world's energy use and greenhouse gas emissions, urban areas are also the main contributors to air, noise, water and land pollution. Moreover, cities generate large quantities of waste, are voracious consumers of natural resources, and they are particularly vulnerable to natural disasters and climate change. Given the current rates of urbanization, the environmental impacts of cities are of urgent concern. This first volume of the series focuses on the effects of urbanization on our planet, analyzing the main environmental challenges that city governments face, and offering a catalog of international urban best practices on environmental issues."

Vol. 2: *Cities and Mobility & Transportation: Towards the next generation of urban mobility,* CreateSpace, 2016.

See, **"Setting the Wheels in Motion for Sustainable Transportation"**. Available at: https://www.amazon.com/dp/1533358141.

"As cities grow, the demand for mobility escalates. This stresses existing urban transport systems and infrastructures, exacerbates widespread traffic, and increases road accidents and fatalities. It also increases greenhouse gas emissions and air and noise pollution, causing serious health concerns and grave environmental repercussions. Thus, ensuring a sustainable and efficient distribution of people, goods and services is essential to cities' social and economic development. This second volume of the series focuses on the main urban mobility and transportation trends and challenges and compiles a catalog of international best practices on sustainable urban mobility."

Vol. 3: *Cities and the Economy: Fueling growth, jobs and innovation,* CreateSpace, 2017.

See, **"Boosting Sustainable Growth via the World's Cities"**. Available at: https://www.amazon.com/dp/1535320818.

"The ability of cities to generate income, employment and well-being for its inhabitants is one of the main drivers behind today's high urbanization rates. As centers of production, innovation, creativity, trade and connectivity, urban areas are taking a leading role in stimulating global economic growth. However, cities can also be places where challenges such as inequality, unemployment, segregation and poverty, are concentrated and exacerbated. This third volume of the series reviews the trends and challenges of economic development in urban areas and debates what city governments can do to foster sustainable urban economic development. In addition, it also highlights international urban best practices fostering economic development and discusses a few notable successful initiatives."

Vol. 4: *Cities and Social Cohesion: Designing more inclusive urban areas,* CreateSpace, 2017.

See, **"From Margin to Center: Fostering Social Cohesion in Cities"**. Available at: https://www.amazon.com/dp/1545000255.

"Cities today are more diverse than ever before – economically, socially, culturally, ethnically and in terms of people's identities and lifestyles. Highly diversified communities can be a source of new opportunities for socio-economic development, social mobility and advanced living standards for citizens and cities around the world. However, they can also create social and economic tensions that result in increasing poverty, inequality, segregation, exclusion, social polarization and insecurity. In fact, social cohesion and inclusion challenges are more intense and visible in cities than any other type of locality. This fourth volume of the series reviews current trends and salient challenges threatening social cohesion in cities and highlights a range of initiatives that cities have launched to reduce urban inequality and increase social inclusion."

Contents

Preface iii
1. Introduction 1
2. Trends and Challenges of Cities in a Globalizing World 3
    The Global City *4*
    2.1. Economic and Financial Flows 7
        2.1.1. Flows of Goods and Services 8
        2.1.2. Flows of Capital and FDI 10
        2.1.3. Air Connectivity 11
    2.2. People Flows 13
        2.2.1 Migration 14
        2.2.2 International Students and Researchers 16
        2.2.3 Tourism 17
            Business Travel *19*
    2.3. Information and Knowledge Flows 26
    2.4 Political Exchange and Global Influence 29
        2.4.1 The Diffusion of State-Power and Decentralization 30
        2.4.2 Geopolitical Opportunities, City Diplomacy and Global Influence 30
            The Proliferation of City Networks *32*
            Cities Engaging in the Global Agenda *40*
    2.5 Perils of Global Cities 42
3. Best Practices and Case Studies of Global Cities 49
    3.1. Global Strategy and International Promotion 52
        3.1.1. City Image, Brand and Reputation 57
    3.2. Trade and Investment 63
    3.3. Attracting and Managing People Flows 72
        3.3.1 Tourism 72

  3.3.2 International Talent 79

  3.3.3 Migration and Refugees 82

 3.4. City's Soft Power Attributes 86

  3.4.1. Culture, Arts and Entertainment 87

  3.4.2 International Events 91

 3.5. Cities as International Actors 93

  City Diplomacy and City Networks 94

  Cities and Political Power 98

4. Concluding Remarks 101

References 105

Appendix I: Additional Resources 117

Appendix II: CIM Index - International Outreach Dimension 119

1. Introduction

Historically, cities have been dynamic centers of economic, political, social and cultural interaction among people from different communities all over the world. From Phoenician cities on the Mediterranean 3,000 years ago; to those along the Silk Road, connecting the East and the West economically and culturally from around 120BC to 1400AC; to modern hubs in the contemporary technology-driven globalization wave. **Throughout time, cities have long been pivotal points of trade, capital and information exchange, linking local, national and global networks.**

Therefore, the phenomenon of cross-border flows of people, goods, capital and knowledge is not new. In fact, the movement of workers, products and ideas has been central to human activity and economic development over centuries. Yet recent policy developments, such as the opening up of national economies and the removal of restrictions to trade, aided by technological change, have sped up the number, intensity and complexity of these connections and interactions to levels never experienced before.

The development of new information and telecommunications technologies (ICTs) has been of critical importance in facilitating connectivity and communications at all levels. This has allowed a greater and deeper number of exchanges, leading to growing global interdependence. Coinciding with this boosted connectivity, **cities and urban areas have become central intersections for global networks**. In fact, one of the main advantages that urban areas have over rural areas is their greater levels of connectivity with the rest of the world.

This new level of urban connectedness has led to economic, political, cultural and societal change, giving cities **a new pivotal role in the architecture of global networks of exchange**. Urban areas are becoming more integrated into the world through expanding networks, which are increasingly centered in and around cities. Therefore, as the lines between the global and the local become more blurred, cities increasingly seek to become more relevant players on a global level. And as the number of people living in cities and the economic power of urban areas both rise, the importance and influence of cities in the global arena will undoubtedly increase. As a result, cities not only demand greater power at the local level, but they also want to be key players on a global scale.

The next part of this book volume, Section 2, provides a short review of the concept "global city," and then emphasizes the increasing role and influence of cities as nodal points in international networks of flows – flows of goods and services, people, and information and culture. This section also looks at the trends and challenges of urban centers at the international level. Section 3 exhibits some initiatives, strategies and case studies of cities adapting themselves to this globalizing age of increasing connectivity. It covers issues such as how metropolises are improving their city image and reputation; strategies to attract talent, trade and investment; and how cities collaborate with each other to be critical actors in global governance; among other topics. The last section of the book offers some concluding thoughts.

***

2. Trends and Challenges of Cities in a Globalizing World

Two megatrends of the 21st century are fueling the global connection of cities as never before: 1) rapid urbanization and 2) globalization characterized by technological change and digitalization. In fact, **the growing number of cities playing relevant roles on the international stage is one of the most important developments of the 21st century**. While some cities – such as New York, London or Tokyo – have long been recognized as "global cities," there were few globally connected cities until quite recently.

This heightened level of global connectivity brings important challenges and opportunities for cities. More connectivity is often related to broader and deeper ties, fostering economic development and innovation, facilitating the sharing of information, minimalizing cultural differences, and increasing cooperation between cities, regions and nations. However, it also increases competition among urban hubs for attracting resources and opportunities. Local governments need to balance the prospects and threats brought by globalization and reap the benefits for society in general and for their citizens in particular.

This section of the book starts with a brief review of the concept "global city" or "world city" and defines its main characteristics. It then exhibits some of the key trends and challenges of cities as nodal points in cross-border flows of people, goods, capital and knowledge, and their increasing role and influence in the international arena.

The Global City

The concept "world city" or "global city" has been a focus of debate since the beginning of the last century. In 1915, Patrick Geddes was one of the first authors who referred to "world cities" in his classic book, *Cities in Evolution*. In 1966, Peter Hall's book, *The World Cities*, described the concept of capturing the different roles performed by cities, such as centers of international trade and financial services, but also of political power, advanced professional activities, scientific knowledge and information (Hall, 2005). Some years later, in 1986, John Friedman was one of the first authors establishing a framework linking urbanization processes and the new global economy, in particular the expanding role of cities as hubs of financial and business services, and establishing a new urban hierarchy in *The World City Hypothesis* (Friedmann, 1986).

However, one of the most prominent authors in the topic is sociologist Saskia Sassen, who popularized the term "global city" in her 1991 book, *The Global City* (Sassen, 1991). She defined global cities as those that function in four ways: (1) as command and control centers of the world economy; (2) as key locations for finance or specialized service firms; (3) as sites of production (including innovations); and (4) as markets of products and innovations (Sassen, 1991).

More recently, the number of authors studying the characteristics and functioning of global cities has multiplied. These authors emphasize diverse aspects of cities' international outreach, as global economic powerhouses, political and cultural hubs of international significance and pivotal centers of people flows. Overall, **"global cities" refer to leading urban centers of economic and political power that are increasingly connected and integrated into global networks of economic, political, human, cultural and information exchanges**. Box 1 summarizes some of the main characteristics that are usually associated with "world cities" and "global cities."

BOX 1. Features of a World City or Global City

- Drivers of the global economy
- Nodes of international trade flows and global value chains (GVCs)
- Key locations for international financial services (e.g. finance, banking, accounting, insurance, real state, etc.)
- Home of several multinational corporations headquarters
- Sites of production and innovations
- Home of great universities and hubs of knowledge and research
- Magnets of human capital and talent
- Political centers with substantial decision-making power and global influence
- Diverse populations in terms of culture, language, religion and ideologies
- International gateways and magnets for migrants
- Cultural, artistic and recreational centers
- Destinations that attract visitors (tourists and international conferences)
- Hubs of information-gathering and diffusion, and nodal points of global communications
- Often large, although not a requirement

Additionally, in recent decades, a number of studies have attempted to identify global cities by ranking their various dimensions. Although the criteria used in these rankings vary[1], we find that some cities such as New York, London, Tokyo, Paris, Hong Kong and Singapore consistently appear in most of the top 10 of global cities rankings (see Table 1). Overall, the increasing interest in global cities research, along with long-term trends of growing connectivity and urbanization rates reflect the rising importance of the global dimension of cities.

---

[1] Some rankings are more centered on cities as global economic powerhouses, while others include different indicators such as human capital, cultural character, information exchanges, political engagement and accessibility.

Table 1. Comparison of a Selection of Global City Indexes – Top 10

City Rank	CIMI 2019 – rank 2018 (IESE)	Globalization and World Cities - GaWC 2018(*)	Global Cities Index 2019 (A.T. Kearney)	Global Power City Index 2018 (MMF)	Global Financial Centers Index 25 - 2019 (Z/Yen and CDI)
1	London	London (Alpha++)	New York	London	New York
2	New York	New York (Alpha++)	London	New York	London
3	Amsterdam	Hong Kong (Alpha+)	Paris	Tokyo	Hong Kong
4	Paris	Beijing (Alpha+)	Tokyo	Paris	Singapore
5	Reykjavík	Singapore (Alpha+)	Hong Kong	Singapore	Shanghai
6	Tokyo	Shanghai (Alpha+)	Singapore	Amsterdam	Tokyo
7	Singapore	Sydney (Alpha+)	Los Angeles	Seoul	Toronto
8	Copenhagen	Paris (Alpha+)	Chicago	Berlin	Zurich
9	Berlin	Dubai (Alpha+)	Beijing	Hong Kong	Beijing
10	Vienna	Tokyo (Alpha+)	Washington, D.C.	Sydney	Frankfurt

Source: Own elaboration based on IESE Cities in Motion 2019 (Berrone and Ricart, 2019), GaWC (2018b); A.T. Kearney (2019); The Mori Memorial Foundation (MMF, 2018); and The Global Financial Centers Index 25 (Z/Yen and CDI, 2019).

Note: (*) The GaWC city classification for 2018 is based upon the magnitude of a city's business service connections to 707 other major cities. It is not a ranking, but rather a classification into levels of world city network integration (Alpha, Beta and Gamma).

***

Chapter 2: Trends and Challenges of Cities

2.1. Economic and Financial Flows

Over the past few decades, **there has been a deep structural transformation in the design and functioning of the global economy,** driven by the spread of globalization, the improvement in transportation systems and the advancement of telecommunication networks. Since the 1970s-1980s, global international trade and foreign direct investment (FDI) flows have increased exponentially, representing a significantly greater share of world's GDP (see Figure 1); financial markets have expanded into global networks; and multinational companies (MNCs) have multiplied around the world, entering new markets and surpassing national economies.

Figure 1: World's Urbanization, Exports and FDI Stocks.

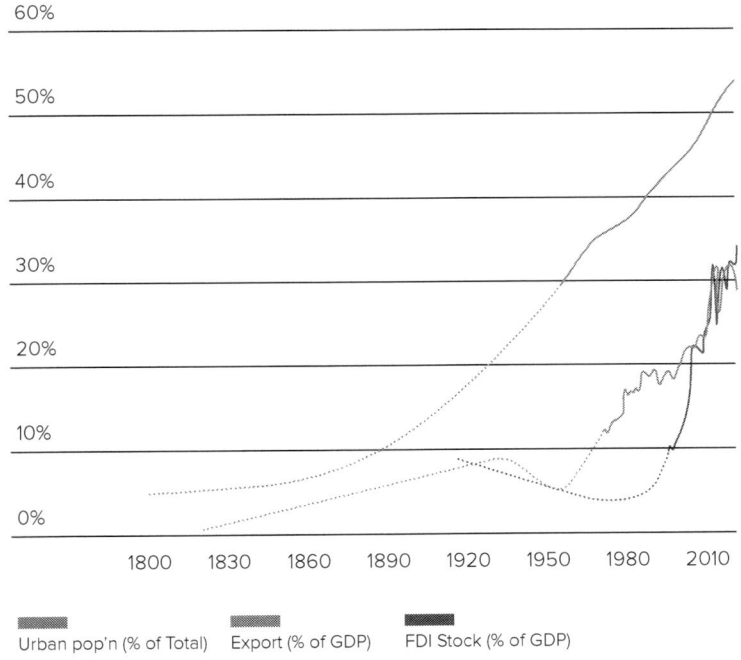

Urban pop'n (% of Total)   Export (% of GDP)   FDI Stock (% of GDP)

Source: DHL Global Connectedness Index 2016 (Ghemawat and Altman, 2016).

Cities have traditionally been gateways to other markets, as they concentrate assets, qualified human resources and better-quality infrastructures. However, as urbanization rates increase, the role of cities as hubs of economic activity and international trade intensifies. **In a globalized economy, where economies are interconnected through international trade and the exchange of resources, cities and regions acquire a new strategic role**. With around 80% of global gross domestic product (GDP) generated in cities, urban areas are the places where most global trade and international investment takes place.

Therefore, **the increasingly robust role of cities and regions in national economies and the global economy is undeniable**. This offers huge opportunities for cities and businesses alike, which now have the opportunity to integrate into the world economy in a way that is unprecedented in scale and scope. However, this shift also results in increasing competition for global resources and capital, such as skilled workers, investments, information flows and tourists that are now moving through these global economic networks.

2.1.1. Flows of Goods and Services

Urban areas have become key hubs or "basing centers" from where MNCs and other institutions and organizations structure and control these economic networks of exchange. Urban areas, and in particular the so-called "global cities," are home to the headquarters of the most powerful transnational corporations; the pivotal points of global value chains (GVC); and the link to global production networks and to international trade.[2] As a result, cities increasingly compete to be strategic locations within these GVCs or specific production networks.

---

[2] *See Vol. 3. Cities and the Economy* (Berrone, Ricart, and Duch T-Figueras, 2017) to know more about the role of cities in the economy.

Chapter 2: Trends and Challenges of Cities

Most countries' exports are increasingly produced and distributed in cities and their metropolitan areas (see Table 2). In fact, **trade flows are increasingly concentrated in a number of economically powerful cities that serve as logistical hubs and distribution networks**. For instance, the world's busiest shipping ports are located in cities, including the ports of Shanghai (China), Singapore (Singapore), Shenzhen (China), Guangzhou (China) and Rotterdam (The Netherlands). Moreover, as the service economy expands, services, and not goods, will be the fastest growing exports in the upcoming decades. High-skilled workers and innovations tend to be concentrated in cities, meaning they will likely be optimally positioned to take advantage of a global services economy.

Table 2. Volume of Exports, Population and GDP in Selected Metropolitan Areas, 2017.

City (Country)	Volume Exports 2017 (US million)	GDP 2017 (US$ million, current prices)	Total Population 2017 (million)
Seoul (South Korea)	406,967	761,835	25.4
Shenzhen (China)	270,042	309,312	11.8
Shanghai (China)	196,291	444,241	25.0
Moscow (Russia)	165,075	414,309	19.9
Paris (France)	107,860	773,748	11.8
Houston (USA)	96,121	496,890	6.8
New York (USA)	94,772	1,731,190	20.2
Hamburg (Germany)	80,324	179,343	3.3
Istanbul (Turkey)	76,254	287,527	15.5
Guangzhou (China)	73,370	308,103	13.5
Barcelona (Spain)	62,996	184,798	5.5
Milan (Italy)	62,315	238,796	4.6
Beijing (China)	59,199	406,911	22.8

Source: [1] Exports: Euromonitor International from national statistics/OECD/International Monetary Fund (IMF), International Financial Statistics (IFS)

[2] GDP: Euromonitor International from national statistics/Eurostat/OECD/UN/ International Monetary Fund (IMF), International Financial Statistics (IFS)

[3] Total Population: Euromonitor International from national statistics/UN

2.1.2. Flows of Capital and FDI

Financial globalization is the process through which financial markets in a given economy become more integrated with those in other economies and the rest of the world through financial flow exchanges. **Cities are the main destinations of flows and stocks of overseas capital and investments**. In fact, some of the first global cities, such as New York, London and Tokyo, are some of the world's leading financial centers. This gives established global cities an advantage when accessing finance, as they often host banks and venture capital firms. Yet secondary cities or smaller cities can also have access to capital flows and foreign direct investment (FDI).

According to fDi's Global City of the Future 2018/2019, Singapore and London have been the top destinations for global foreign direct investment, accounting for almost 5% of all investment since 2003 (fDi Intelligence - Financial Times, 2019). Table 3 shows the top 25 cities in the world for attracting FDI in 2018, with Singapore at the top position. However, Singapore might be a special case since it is both a city and a nation-state.

The rest of the Top 25 exhibits a little bit of concentration of FDI attractiveness in certain parts of the world, especially in developed countries - 10 out of the 25 cities are in Europe, and seven in North America. However, we can also observe some emerging market cities, such as in Beijing or Shanghai, as well as cities of different sizes, exhibiting that cities of different characteristics have the potential to take advantage of capital flows and FDI attraction.

Structural factors such as human capital, connectivity and the ease of doing business are important for companies when choosing investment locations. However, local governments and subnational investment promotion agencies have the potential to maximize the economic and social characteristics of a city to attract investments, as we will see in Section 3.

Table 3. Top 25 FDI's Global City of the Future 2018/2019

Rank	City, Country	Rank	City, Country
1	Singapore, Singapore	14	Belfast, UK
2	London, UK	15	Helsinki, Finland
3	Dublin, Ireland	16	Seoul, South Korea
4	Hong Kong, Hong Kong	17	Montreal, Canada
5	Shanghai, China	18	Seattle, US
6	Dubai, UAE	19	Beijing, China
7	New York, US	20	Copenhagen, Denmark
8	Amsterdam, Netherlands	21	Sydney, Australia
9	San Francisco, US	22	Munich, Germany
10	Tokyo, Japan	23	Toronto, Canada
11	Paris, France	24	Houston, US
12	Frankfurt, Germany	25	Miami, US
13	Zurich, Switzerland		

Source: fDi's Global City of the Future 2018/19

2.1.3. Air Connectivity

Connectivity is crucial for a city's development as it has a direct impact on the local economy through a variety of channels, including international trade, FDI, tourism and migration. Despite the difficulties in measuring a city's connectivity level, air connectivity can be a good proxy of economic activity and economic growth to some extent, because air connectivity enables a city to attract investment and human capital and to trade and exchange with other localities. Increasing air connectivity also facilitates the flow of people, as exhibited in the next section.

Global air connectivity has grown remarkably in recent decades, thanks to technology advances, improvements in infrastructures and growing efficiencies in the aviation sector. Distances between cities, at both national and international levels, seem shorter than ever, easing the movement of goods and people. **Cities such as London, Paris, Frankfurt, Istanbul and Dubai are among the world's most globally connected cities by air.** From these urban hubs, you can reach over 200 international destinations through direct city-to-city flights (see Table 4). From the six international airports of the city of London, for instance, you can reach more than 300 international locations, making the UK's capital one of the most connected and accessible cities in the world.

Table 4. The World's Most Connected Cities (air connectivity), 2016 – Top 15

Rank	City, Country	Number of connexions
1	London, UK	351
2	Paris, France	291
3	Frankfurt am Main, Germany	278
4	Amsterdam, Netherlands	242
5	Istanbul, Turkey	239
6	Munich, Germany	217
7	Brussels, Belgium	214
8	Dubai, UAE	213
9	Rome, Italy	184
10	Düsseldorf, Germany	175
11	Vienna, Austria	167
12	Milan, Italy	163
13	Zürich, Switzerland	162
14	Manchester, UK	162
15	Moscow, Russia	160

Source: Rome2rio Global Connectivity Ranking, 2016.

Note: Ranking reflects the number of international cities that a city is connected to through direct flights (i.e. connections city to city, not airport to airport.)

Note 2: The ranking was computed using Rome2rio's global transit data from April 2014 to January 2016.

***

2.2. People Flows

Today, with the improvement of transportation systems and increases in income per capita level, international mobility has become easier and more accessible than ever before. For instance, with a more competitive aviation sector, as previously mentioned, and more people entering middle-class populations, annual growth in global air traffic passenger demand has been consistently positive since 2006 (with the exception of the year 2009), with an average annual growth in global air traffic passenger demand from 2006 to 2019 of almost 6% (Statista, 2019). Moreover, on a global scale, passenger air travel is expected to experienced sustained growth rates in the coming years. (See Figure 2.)

Figure 2. Number of Airport Passengers by City in 2018 (in millions) – Top 20

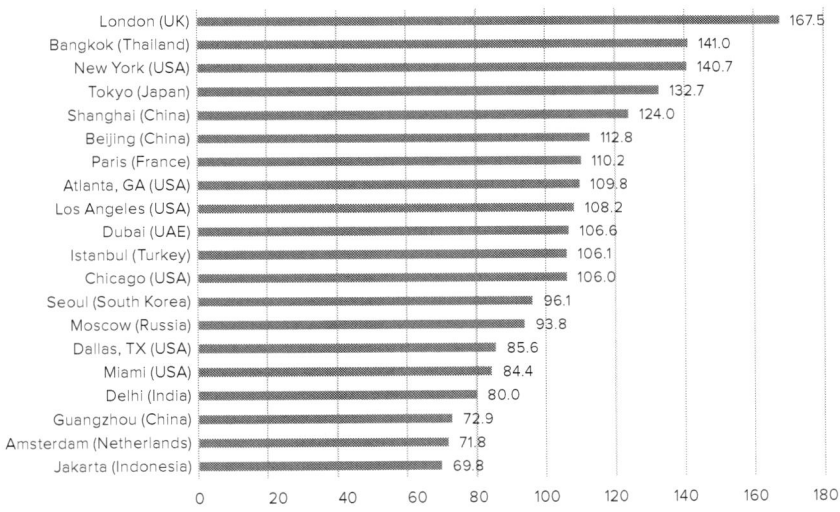

Source: Own elaboration with data from Euromonitor International from national statistics/American Public Transportation Association/City Public Transport Authorities.

Note: Refers to the number of inbound and outbound passengers of airports within the metropolitan area of respective city. On some occasions, numbers include passengers in airports adjacent to metropolitan area. Both scheduled and charter flights are included.

Managing human mobility is one of the biggest challenges for cities today, both in developed and developing countries. The causes and motivations of human mobility can be very different, thus resulting in different actions needed by the government. People flows can be long term, as in the case of migration; medium term, with international students, international researchers and professionals; or short term, as in the case of tourists or people travelling for business.

2.2.1 Migration

Migration flows can be internal, with populations moving within the same country, mainly from rural areas to urban areas, but also between cities of the same country. They can also be international, with citizens moving across international borders. Migration is increasingly voluntary, with people seeking opportunities and a better quality of life. But it may also be involuntary, as in the case of refugees, asylum seekers and internally displaced people (IDPs).

Migration flows are one of the most pressing challenges and intensely debated political issues of our time. It is estimated that there were 763 million internal migrants in 2013 and some 244 million international migrants in 2015 worldwide (WEF, 2017). From 2000 to 2015, annual migration grew 2.4%, outpacing annual population growth of 1.2% (WEF, 2017). At the international level, the percentage of people living outside the countries they were born has risen from 2.9% in 2005 to 3.3% in 2015. This reflects an increasing tendency, although still a limited one, as it represents just 3% of the overall population (Ghemawat and Altman, 2016).

Cities, particularly those considered world cities, are the principal destination points of international migrants. **It is estimated that around 19% of the world's foreign-born populations live in global cities** (IOM, 2015). In some cities, such as Dubai and Brussels, more than 50 percent of the population is foreign-born. In other well-known world cities, including Sydney, Los Angeles, Singapore, London and New York, more than one-third of the population was born in another country (IOM, 2015). However, migration in the future will most likely increase most significantly in cities within countries that have emerging economies, such as South Africa, Brazil and India. Countries in Southeast Asia, as well as in secondary cities in the developed world, are also experiencing surges in foreign-born populations (Armbrecht, 2016). (See Figure 3.)

Figure 3: Foreign Citizens as Percentage of Total Population in 2005, 2011 and 2017 in Selected Cities (%)

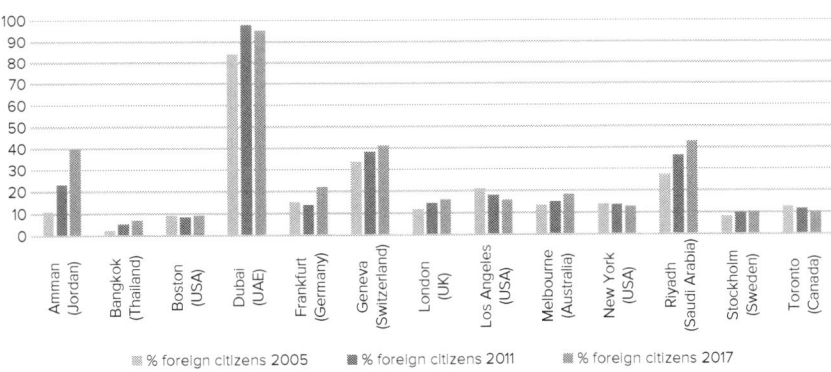

Source: Own elaboration with data from Euromonitor International.
Note: Foreign citizens are those who reside in the city, but are citizens of another country.

As a result, **city leaders and urban managers are increasingly accountable as first responders to the needs and pressures resulting from migration flows**. Nonetheless, migration polices are often still regulated at national and international levels, bringing important challenges to city leaders. Significant levels of migrations into cities can bring important challenges for city leaders, such as integration and social cohesion problems[3];

---

[3] See book volume *Cities and Social Cohesion* (Berrone, Ricart, and Duch, 2017) for additional information on the immigration challenge and its consequences to social cohesion in cities.

housing and infrastructure deficits, resulting in a high number of people living in slums, especially in developing countries; transport and mobility challenges; education, employment and health deficits; and safety and security problems. However, migration flows also tend to result in highly diverse cities, which can lead to higher levels of creativity, thus triggering innovation and economic development. Therefore, migration can be a powerful tool for prosperity.

The recent refugee crisis has also shown how cities are often the first point of arrival for refugees and asylum seekers. For instance, it is estimated that Europe alone will have to accommodate more than 500,000 new immigrants annually in the following years, most of whom will establish their base points in cities (WEF, 2017). Cities such as Athens, Budapest, Genoa, Munich and Vienna have become transit hubs for refugees who aim to relocate to other countries, posing important challenges to these cities.

2.2.2 International Students and Researchers

International students, foreign scholars and researchers – that is, "international talent" – are also contributors to the local economy and a source of new ideas, creativity and research and development. **Cities and regions are entering into a global competition to attract, develop and retain international talent**. For instance, a recent study by QS Top Universities ranks London (#1), Tokyo (#2), Melbourne (#3), Montreal (#4) and Paris (#5) as the 2018 best cities in the world for international students, due their leading universities, job markets, diversity and cultural offer, among other factors.

Enhancing a city's attractiveness in order to draw international skilled labor, creative talent and entrepreneurs is increasingly part of a city's international strategy, an issue that will be analyzed in the book volume *Cities and Human Capital*.

As we will discuss in Section 3, cities are strengthening their strategies to build their brands and their reputations to attract talent. Moreover, urban areas and regions around the world increasingly strive to ensure a soft landing and positive integration of this talent.

2.2.3 Tourism

The World Tourism Organization (UNWTO) defines tourists as people "traveling to and staying in places outside their usual environment for not more than one consecutive year for leisure, business and other purposes" (UNWTO, 1995). Since the mid-20th century, tourism has experienced an exponential and continuous growth, becoming one of the fastest rising and largest economic sectors in the world, and a key driver for socio-economic progress.

In 2017, the tourism industry growth outpaced overall global economy growth for the seventh successive year (WTTC, 2018). The tourism business today equals or even surpasses other important economic sectors such as oil exports, food products and automobiles (UNWTO, 2017b). Also in 2017, the travel & tourism industry contributed US$8.3 trillion to the global economy (10.4% of global GDP) and generated some 313 million jobs (or 9.9% of total employment)[4] (WTTC, 2018). The sector is expected to continue growing, generating US$12.4 trillion and generating over 413 million jobs by 2028 (Ibid).

International tourism, in particular, has seen remarkable growth. In 1950, there were 25 million international tourist arrivals globally. In 2017, this number was 50 times larger, with 1.3 billion international arrivals globally (UNWTO, 2018).[5] (See Figure 4.) This striking growth of international tourism has been driven by rises in income per capita levels; improvements in the

---

[4] Between direct and indirect jobs.

[5] Europe was the world's most visited region in the world (with 51% of all international tourist arrivals), followed by Asia and the Pacific (25%).

transportation sector and decreasing travel costs; and advancements in ICTs and other technologies. As one of the main actors in international commerce, tourism represented 7% of the world's exports in 2016, with a total value of up to US$1.4 trillion in 2016 (UNWTO, 2017a). International travelers from China, United States and Germany, in this order, were among the biggest tourism spenders worldwide in 2017 (UNWTO, 2018).

Figure 4. International Tourism, 1990-2016

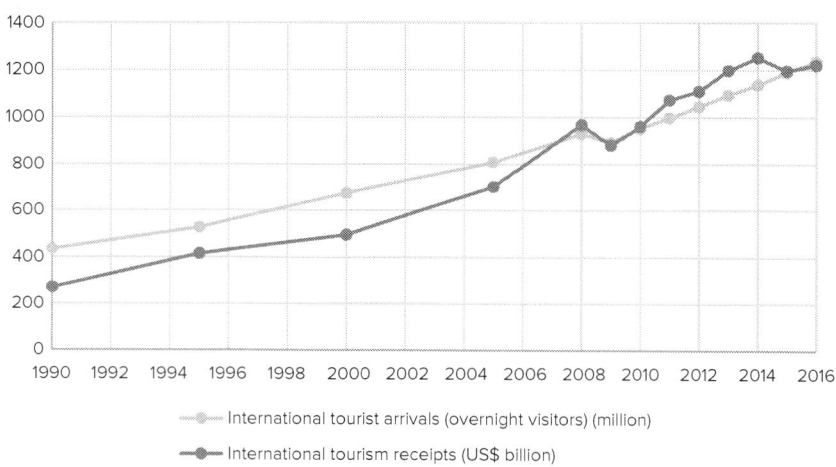

Source: Own elaboration with data from World Tourism Organization (UNWTO, 2017a).

The unprecedented rise of global tourism is having a great impact on nations and cities alike. Cities have gradually grown as key tourist destinations and **urban tourism has become one of the fastest- growing types of tourism**. Between 2007 and 2014, the number of city trips increased by 82%, reaching a 22% share of all holidays (IPK International, 2016). In 2016, the top 100 cities accounted for 558 million international arrivals (Euromonitor International, 2017b). In Europe, for instance, the so-called "city-breaks" – 48 hours of urban tourism – have risen significantly, mainly due to the growth of budget airlines and changes in people's preferences.

Growth in urban tourism is experienced by cities embedded in both developed and emerging economies. (See Table 5.) In particular, Asian cities are on the rise. The city of Bangkok was one of the most visited cities in the world in 2017, with around 20 million visitors who spent some US$16.36 billion in the city (Mastercard, 2018). Other cities in the top 10 of the most popular city destinations with over 10 million international visitors in 2017 were London, Paris, Dubai, Singapore, New York, Kuala Lumpur, Tokyo and Istanbul.

Table 5: Virtuous Circle of Tech Hubs in Global Cities

#	City, Country	2017 International Overnight Visitors (Millions)
1	Bangkok, Thailand	20.05
2	London, UK	19.83
3	Paris, France	17.44
4	Dubai, UAE	15.79
5	Singapore, Singapore	13.91
6	New York, USA	13.13
7	Kuala Lumpur, Malaysia	12.58
8	Tokyo, Japan	11.93
9	Istanbul, Turkey	10.70
10	Seoul, South Korea	9.54
11	Antalya, Turkey	9.42
12	Phuket, Thailand	9.29
13	Makkah, Saudi Arabia	9.18
14	Hong Kong, China	9.03
15	Milan, Italy	8.81

Source: Own elaboration.
Note: The 2018 Mastercard Destination Cities Index includes 162 cities.

Business Travel

Although leisure travel is still the main purpose for travelling, with just over half of all international tourists worldwide travelling for leisure purposes, around 13% of all inbound international tourists reported travelling for business and professional purposes in 2016 (UNWTO, 2017a).[6] Therefore, business travel or professional tourism is an important part of the tourism industry. In fact, global business travel spending generated 22.5% of direct Travel & Tourism GDP in 2017, or US$1.2 trillion, and it is predicted to rise to US$1.8 trillion by 2028 (WTTC, 2018).

Business travel involves all travel-related activities and expenses linked to conferences, conventions, congresses, exhibitions, international fairs and all kind of meetings and professional events. **Cities tend to host a relatively large amount of these business meetings and professional events**. Due to the potential economic benefits of these events, cities around the world, especially in developed and emerging countries, compete to become magnets for business travelers and host international meeting and events (See Table 6.)

Table 6. Top 10 Cities by Number of International Association Meetings in 2018

Rank	City	# Meetings
1	Paris, France	212
2	Vienna, Austria	172
3	Madrid, Spain	165
4	Barcelona, Spain	163
5	Berlin, Germany	162
6	Lisbon, Portugal	152
7	London, UK	150
8	Singapore, Singapore	145
9	Prague, Czech Republic	136
10	Bangkok, Thailand	135

Note: This data only includes association meetings taking place regularly, rotating between at least three countries, and with at least 50 participants.
Source: International Congress and Convention Association (ICCA, 2019).

[6] Another 27% travelled for other reasons such as visiting friends and relatives, religious reasons, health treatment, etc.; and the remaining 7% did not specify the purpose of their visit.

Tourism, both for leisure and business, has become a key pillar for economic growth and prosperity in cities: it creates jobs, increases revenues across sectors (transportation, accommodation, food and beverages, retail, culture, arts and entertainment, etc.), triggers innovation and promotes investment in infrastructures and services provision. Consequently, many cities around the world consider the development of urban tourism as an opportunity for economic development, employment generation and urban change.

However, a high influx of tourists has an important impact on local economies and the lives of residents. **If the benefits and drawbacks of city tourism are not carefully considered and balanced urban development is not achieved, global tourism can result in significant economic, social, environmental and spatial negative consequences for the city and its citizens.** As city tourism is expected to continue growing in the upcoming years, cities will face tremendous challenges when seeking to manage the negative effects of tourism, including over-tourism, mobility, security and safety and sustainability challenges.

First, **if the growth of mass-tourism is not well managed, it can result in overcrowding or "overtourism."** Overtourism describes "destinations where hosts or guests, locals or visitors, feel that there are too many visitors and that the quality of life in the area or the quality of the experience has deteriorated unacceptably" (Goodwin, 2017).[7] Overtourism can result in over-use of infrastructure and space; mobility and transportation challenges; rising costs of housing and living; gentrification or "touristification"; segregation and social exclusion; and an overall deterioration of the quality of life of the local residents.

A number of current dynamics and developments, such as the rapid growth of low-cost aviation, the rise of the cruise ship industry and peer-to-peer home sharing platforms, all play roles in exacerbating the problem

---

[7] This is the opposite of responsible tourism or sustainable tourism, by which tourism improves the overall quality of life of the city or the location.

of overtourism. Several cities around the world, such as Barcelona, Venice or Amsterdam, are struggling with overtourism (See Box 2). Local residents of these cities, and of other cities affected by overtourism, are becoming increasingly vocal about their dissatisfaction with tourism, protesting these massive influxes of tourists and demanding solutions and initiatives to counterbalance the negative impacts of mass tourism.

> **BOX 2. The Challenges of Overtourism in Cities: A Growing Global Problem**
>
> As previously mentioned, cities are increasingly becoming destination hubs for the growing number of tourists around the world. Some European cities, such as Barcelona, Amsterdam, Venice, Santorini, Paris, Rome, and more recently Lisbon and Prague, are struggling with massive numbers of tourists overcrowding city centers. Overtourism occurs when local citizens feel that the number of tourists affects the quality of life. Problems of anti-social behavior, such as vandalism or night noise, often accompany overtourism.
>
> Protests against overtourism have taken place in a number of European cities in recent years, aiming to "reclaim the city." This has led to the creation of organizations such as the Assembly of Neighborhoods for Sustainable Tourism (ABTS) and the Network of Southern European Cities against tourism (SET), which aim to fight overtourism and the impact it has on local residents (Cheer, Novelli, and Milano, 2018).
>
> **Venice**
>
> Venice is widely considered one of the first cases of city overtourism. In 2017, 9.5 million tourists visited Venice, accounting for 37 million overnights (Venezia today, 2018). With a population of just 260,000 people (55,000 living in the historic center, where most of the tourists concentrate), the City of Canals has been struggling with problems of overcrowding and tensions between locals and tourists for years. The rise of the day-tripper has only worsened the problem. For instance, on some days as many as 44,000 cruise ship passengers enter the city (Responsible Travel, n.d.). The overcrowding of tourists not only affects the quality of life of Venetians, but also the city's economy (it is increasingly difficult to find employment outside the tourism sector), and a rise in the overall cost of living (food, transport, property, etc.). In fact, the number of Venetians living in the city center has dropped from 120,000 three decades ago to 55,000 today (Responsible Travel, n.d.).

Tourists in Venice

In response to this situation, the Mayor of Venice since 2015 Luigi Brugnaro introduced a number of measures to reduce the number of tourists in certain areas of the city. For instance, a marketing campaign, #EnjoyRespectVenezia, was launched to encourage positive behavior among tourists, as well as reinforce a number of rules and regulations, with potential fines of up to 500€ for littering, picnics in public areas, swimming in canals, or using noisy wheeled suitcases. Additionally, cruise ships over 55,000 tons will be banned from entering St. Mark's Basin and the Giudecca Canal starting in 2021, while temporary regulations have been put in place to redirect tourists away from some areas (Responsible Travel, n.d.).

Barcelona

Since the Barcelona Olympic Games in 1992, tourism in the Catalan capital has boomed. In 1990, Barcelona received 1.7 million tourists, accounting for 3.8 million overnights. In 2017, these numbers had risen to 8.9 million tourists coming to the city, accounting for 18.8 million overnights (Ajuntament de Barcelona, 2017). Thus, the number of tourists and overnights in the city area has quintupled in less than 30 years. At the greater metropolitan level, Barcelona received more than 11 million tourists, accounting for 30 million overnights in 2017 (Ajuntament de Barcelona, 2017).

Barcelona's rapid growth in tourism, especially during peak season periods, has triggered many concerns and complaints from local citizens. Protests across the city have been increasing, especially in neighborhoods most impacted by tourism, such as Barceloneta and Ciutat Vella. Locals argue that rental prices have increased, mainly due to the proliferation of licensed and unlicensed tourist apartments, and complain about the anti-social behaviors of party-seeking visitors.

Barcelona, Spain

In order to try to find a solution for the situation, Barcelona's town hall has implemented a number of measures to try to control the negative effects of over-tourism. For example, it has placed a temporary moratorium on new hotels and has tried to limit the growth of vacation rentals by taking actions against illegal apartments that draw tourists. In June 2018, Airbnb and the Barcelona City Council reached an agreement in which Airbnb committed to sharing data with Barcelona officials about listings on their online platform (Congostrina, 2018). In this way, the city officials can track host ID numbers and apartments listed and check to see if those apartments have the license to operate. If the owner of the apartment does not have a license, the city will demand withdrawal of the unlicensed apartment from the online platform and a substantial fine may be issued.

Amsterdam

Amsterdam also struggles with massive influxes of visitors coming to the city every year. With a population of some 850,000 people, in 2016, the city received 7.3 arrivals accounting for almost 14 million overnight stays (Municipality of Amsterdam, 2018). Therefore, it is one of the European cities with the highest number of tourists per inhabitant.

As with the previous two cases, Amsterdam is looking for ways to control the number of people coming to the city center. The city has banned the opening of new tourist shops, such as souvenir shops, and new eateries tailored almost exclusively to tourists, such as crepe stands. It has also established fines for some anti-social behaviors, such as drinking alcohol on the streets. Moreover, the city has also plans to ban Airbnb short-term rentals in busy areas, divert cruise ships from docking in the city center, and crack down on "fun rides" like Segways, beer bikes and boozy boat trips (Traveller AU, 2018).

The Amsterdam city council is taking an innovative approach by using new technologies. The "I am Amsterdam" team (from the tourism office) has analyzed the tourist movement patterns through data stored on the chip inside Amsterdam's City Card. They have then sought to change these patterns, so that fewer people are in the same place at the same time (Coffey, 2017). An app, called "Discover the City", sends users notifications warnings when an attraction is busier than usual and proposes alternatives, so that tourists are redistributed across the city (Ibid). This has been complemented with a strategy to rebrand places outside the city center in order to redistribute the high influx of people coming to the city center. Through these initiatives, the city is experimenting with creative ways to overcome the challenge of overtourism.

Amsterdam, Netherlands.

Moreover, the rise of global tourism also poses important challenges to cities such as safety and security. For instance, as urban areas grow in importance and influence, and become magnets for tourists and people in general, cities have become primary locations for transnational violence and terrorism. Some of the most worldwide known cities, such as New

York, Madrid, Brussels, Paris, London and Barcelona, have become targets of terrorist attacks in the past decades.

Overall, tourism has the potential to benefit the cities' local economies and the socio-economic conditions of its citizens. However, **local authorities play a key role managing the opportunities and pitfalls brought by tourism in cities, so that it does not result in a loss of quality of life for locals**. Implementing the right policies, with long-term planning and a vision; making accurate investment decisions; creating high-quality jobs; ensuring benefits are distributed across society; and carrying out a collaborative process that involves all stakeholders and citizens are crucial strategies for local administrations dealing with mass tourism. Section 3 will analyze some best practices and actions that some cities are implementing to boost sustainable tourism.

***

2.3. Information and Knowledge Flows

The sharing of ideas and information between and through different people or countries, also known as *social globalization*, is not a new phenomenon. However, technological changes, in particular the spread of digital technology and the exponential growth of internet connectivity, have facilitated and multiplied the number and expansion of global flows of knowledge, ideas and information. In fact, the continued development of ICT infrastructure is enabling the transition from a global economy based on agriculture and industry to one centered on service and information.

Today, around two-thirds of the world's population have mobile phones. In 2017, 48% of the world's population used the internet, up from 16% of total population in 2005 (ITU, 2017).[8] Moreover, **cross-border data flows are skyrocketing**. According to a report by McKinsey, cross-border data flows accounted for US$2.8 trillion of global GDP in 2014, generating more economic value than traditional flows of traded goods (Manyika et al., 2016). These are just some figures reflecting the increasing importance of digital technologies and ICTs. Although issues related to data flows and new technologies will be analyzed further in the future book volume *Cities and Technology*, it is worth mentioning here. Cities, as nodes of connectivity of these information networks, are progressively having a more relevant role facilitating these economic and social exchanges. The spread of new digital technologies and the ubiquity of internet connectivity are reconfiguring the interactions taking place in the global arena, and **with the rise of the "information society," urban centers become the physical enablers of global connectivity**.

Moreover, cities have higher human capital (both stocks and inflows) and generate more knowledge outcomes (innovation, patents, copyrights, etc.). As a result, because cities are the main points of access to connectivity networks, and global hubs of talent and capital, **urban areas are becoming the global centers of information, innovation and knowledge creation**. In this context, cities emerge as clusters of knowledge and education on the one hand, and as the "new centers of technological innovation" on the other. Regarding the former, global cities form global networks through clusters of top universities, the international circulation of faculty and students, and scientific collaborations (Saskia Sassen et al., n.d.). Knowledge and education are crucial resources in today's information economy, and cities that are able to attract international students, researchers and innovative companies will be better positioned to develop their economies and talent.

---

[8] This proportion was significantly higher for the youth (aged 15-24) reaching some 71% of them using the Internet.

Chapter 2: Trends and Challenges of Cities

Additionally, **cities are becoming the world's main "tech hubs."** A tech hub can be defined as a physical space, area or community that fosters innovation for technology start-ups and technological companies. Silicon Valley, in California (USA), is probably the best well-known example, but there are many more successful tech hubs around the world, such as London's Silicon Roundabout, Boston's Route 128, and other cities with a well-established technological start-ups and innovation scene, including New York, Barcelona, Berlin and Cape Town, among others.

These "tech hub" cities are usually global cities, too. A well-developed high-tech industry and innovation sector tends to be accompanied by growth and employment, which improves the image and reputation of a city. However, there are some exceptions, such as in the case San Francisco and Silicon Valley, which have been associated lately with growing inequality, rising costs of living, gentrification and deepening poverty in some parts of society. Nevertheless, in general, one may say that tech hub cities are associated with a positive image and reputation, which in turn attract more talent and human capital. All this contributes to the improvement and expansion of those tech hubs (See Figure 5.)

Figure 5: Virtuous Circle of Tech Hubs in Global Cities

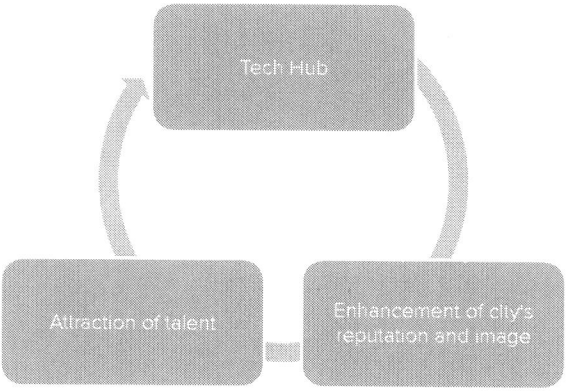

Source: Own elaboration.

Overall, **innovative cities tend to be open cities – open to new ideas, new talent, and disruptive innovations. This results in greater levels of innovation coming to and emerging in the city**. Therefore, knowledge hub cities and "star" tech hub cities are often associated with a more positive and enhanced global city image. All of these ideas will be further developed in the book volume *Cities and Human Capital*. However, it is important to highlight the role of knowledge, technology and innovation in reinforcing the image and reputation of a global city. This, in turn, attracts human capital, leading to the generation of technological innovation and a more positive reputation of the urban hub as a global city.

***

2.4 Political Exchange and Global Influence

World urbanization, increasing connectivity, and economic and social integration are resulting in a paradigm shift with major transformative realignments. In today's multi-dimensional, hyper-connected and interdependent world, power and influence have become more diffuse. As the limits between the local and the global become increasingly blurred, a new balance of power between non-state actors, cities, national governments, supra-national bodies and citizens' networks and organizations arises.

Cities, as centers of people, resources and economic power, are reshaping the new evolving world order in two different ways: first, through the decentralization of state power; and second, by raising the role and scope of influence of cities on a global scale.

2.4.1 The Diffusion of State Power and Decentralization

Some policy areas, such as public health, job creation, mobility, environment or education, to name a few, are usually thought to be national domains. However, all of these have a direct effect on the quality of life and well-being of city dwellers. Local administrations, as the closest level of government to citizens, are often better positioned to understand the needs and demands of their citizens and to offer better solutions.

As urban areas grow in size and power, and digital transformations facilitate communication and exchanges, mayors and city managers around the world are demanding to become more relevant actors in policymaking and governance. Cities want to take action. **As new forms of governance and decision-making tools appear, local governments are demanding for more decentralization and greater autonomy to give their citizens more tailored responses to local and global challenges**. More precisely, it is crucial to decentralize politics in the areas where there is a lack of political power for cities, but that significantly affect them.

In order to increase the role of cities to respond to problems more effectively, city leaders need more autonomy, decision-making capabilities and power. New governance structures and new systems of organization more relevant to today's world configuration need to be established in order to make this happen.

2.4.2 Geopolitical Opportunities, City Diplomacy and Global Influence

The current international system is characterized by global interdependence. And **cities are at the heart of this global interdependence**. From environmental issues and climate change, to international trade and finance, migration or global security, these are all some of the most pressing global challenges of the 21st century, whose effects and consequences are local.

As a result, city governments not only want and need more power at the local level, but they also want to be key players in the international arena. City governments want to become active actors in dealing with and solving these global challenges; and they want to take part in the international agenda, so as to have the capacity to impact local, regional and global policy in order to drive the city's agenda and to meet the needs of their citizens.

Increasing connectivity is allowing new and incumbent actors to connect and interact. Because of this hyper-connectivity, **the scope of influence and power of cities in the international arena is being transformed**. For instance, diplomacy, which has traditionally been thought of as an activity designated only to nation-states[9], is increasingly becoming a strategic activity for cities around the world. In fact, **a main challenge for city managers worldwide is to be able to act more strategically in the international arena in order to become a more relevant actor in the realm of global governance**.

But cities' resources differ from those of states. As a result, they must make use of different tools. For instance, one possible approach is to create an international office within the city council specifically dedicated to international strategy. However, a crucial tool for cities is their ability to collaborate with other cities and act in a coordinated manner. Only by effective cooperation, with concrete actions and goals, will cities be able to achieve their foreign policy goals and gain voice in international forums in which they were previously underrepresented. In this regard, new forms of **city-to-city ("trans-municipal") collaboration** such as **city-to-city networks** or **sister cities / twin cities partnerships** can be powerful tools for policy exchange and international engagement. All of these types of cross border

---

[9] Although diplomacy already existed before the emergence of states, with ancient city-states like Athens or Italian-city states like Venice already establishing diplomatic relations abroad with other territories, today's system of international relations is a legacy of the 17th-century Westphalian political institutions, where diplomacy is commonly understood as a responsibility solely to nations (Chan, 2016).

cooperation among local governments have increased considerably in past decades and have dealt with a wide range of global issues (See Figure 6.)

Figure 6: Cities' Strategies to City Diplomacy

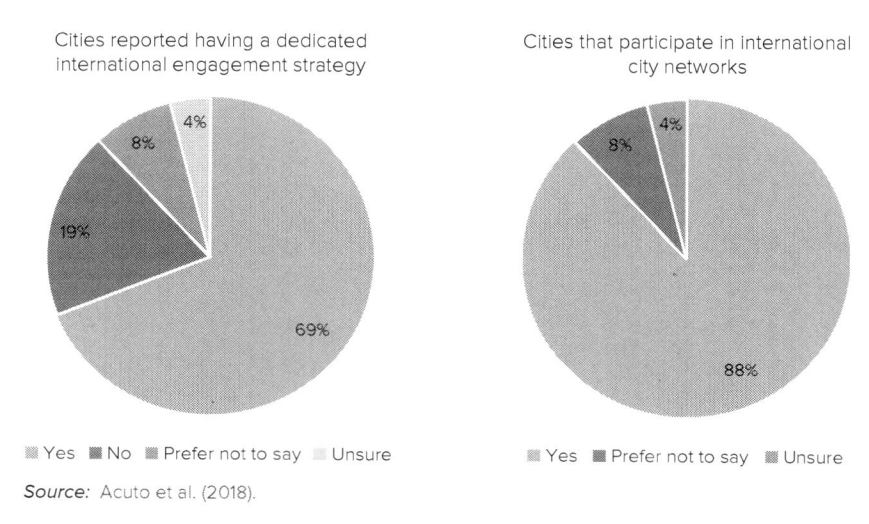

Cities reported having a dedicated international engagement strategy

- Yes 69%
- No 19%
- Prefer not to say 8%
- Unsure 4%

Cities that participate in international city networks

- Yes 88%
- Prefer not to say 8%
- Unsure 4%

Source: Acuto et al. (2018).

The Proliferation of City Networks

As cities grow in size and power, local governments around the world are joining forces to formally organize themselves to cooperate among them and to make their voices heard. As a result, cities have begun to set up networks for cooperation and information exchange, such as city networks and urban platforms and associations. In recent years, city-to-city networks have proliferated around the world in a variety of forms and objectives. **Today, there are hundreds of formalized city networks globally addressing a wide range of issues at different levels** (Acuto et al., 2018).

Urban networks have been initiated at all levels: *sub-national* (e.g. Municipal Association of Victoria, Australia); *national* (e.g. FEMP –

Federación Española de Municipios y Provincias (Spanish Federation of municipalities and provinces) or the National League of Cities, USA); *regional* (e.g. *Mercociudades* in South America); or at the *international* level (e.g. UCLG, Metropolis). There are also networks led by international institutions and agencies, such as the Kitakyushu Initiative for a Clean Environment, led by the UNESCAP; and networks sponsored by large philanthropic foundations, such as the 100 Resilient Cities, pioneered by The Rockefeller Foundation. A study by Acuto and Rayner (2016), which reviews a database of 170 city networks in 2015, found that some 49% of urban networks were national state-based organizations; regional city networks accounted for 21% of total city networks; international networks accounted for 29% of the total; and subnational networks represented the remaining 1%. Therefore, cities are still related substantially to national governments (Acuto and Rayner, 2016).

In regards to city networks at the international level, the International Union of Local Authorities (IULA) - also known as the *Union internationale des villes et pouvoirs locaux* - was the first global local government association ever created, founded in 1913 (City Mayors Archive, n.d.). The IULA aimed at promoting democratic local self-government worldwide. Since then, and in particular since the 1990s and the beginning of the 2000s, the number of local government international networks has risen exponentially. One of the largest global associations representing local governance is the United Cities and Local Governments (UCLG), a network that represents and defends the interests of more than 2,400 towns, cities, regions and metropolises on the world stage.[10] Another well-known city network example is Metropolis, an international city network that focuses on giving a voice to big conurbations, representing the authorities of 137 major cities and their metropolitan areas worldwide. Additionally, we can find city networks dedicated to increasing their influence in regional policymaking,

---

[10] UCLG resulted from the merger of IULA and World Federation of Unities Cities (FMCU-UTO).

such as Eurocities, a network of major European cities aimed at putting the issue of cities and their economic, political and social development onto the European agenda.

Some international city networks focus on a particular issue or policy area. **Issue-specific international city networks** take aim at areas such as the environment and sustainability (see Section 3.5). For instance, the C40 Group (The Cities Climate Leadership Group), an assembly of more than 90 cities around the world committed to fighting climate change, or ICLEI (Local Governments for Sustainability), a global network of more than 1,500 cities, towns and regions working to build sustainable futures, are two big and influential associations. We can also find city networks centered on other issues or themes, such as mobility, with the Cities for Mobility, a worldwide network for urban mobility; or on culture, with the World Cities Culture Forum. Cities are also engaging directly with international organizations and supranational bodies such as The Resilient Cities Group at the World Bank or the Committee of the Regions at the European Union. And there are also associations of mayors, such as the Global Parliament of Mayors, a governance body of, by and for mayors all around the world who seek to overcome global problems with a local impact.

Lastly, city networks not only vary by their level of government and scope, they also diverge greatly by their number of members. Some networks have many members (e.g. ICLEI reports more than 1,500 cities, towns and regions as members), while others have a smaller number (e.g. UCCI - *Unión de Ciudades Capitales Iberoamericanas*, with only 30 members). They also differ in terms of the type of members in their networks, with traditional networks formed by cities only, and others by cities and city associations, or even NGOs and the private sector as part of the network. Therefore, **the current system of global city networks is extremely varied and complex, with multiple platforms and initiatives,**

varying in size, scope and membership. A summary of city networks at global and regional levels is shown in Tables 7A and 7B.[11]

Table 7A. A Selection of City Networks at the Global Level

City network	Scope	Number of members (as of 2018)
100 Resilient Cities (www.100resilientcities.org)	Founded by the Rockefeller Foundation, aims at helping cities to become more resilient to the physical, social and economic challenges of the 21st century.	Around 100 cities
AIMF – International Association of Francophone Mayors (www.aimf.asso.fr)	Sustainable and shared growth of cities in French-speaking countries.	290+ Capital cities, major cities and national local authority associations in 51 countries
AIVP (www.aivp.org)	Port Cities	+160 public and private development stakeholders
C40 Network (www.c40.org)	To address climate change	90+ megacities
Cities Alliance (www.citiesalliance.org)	To promote and strengthen the role of cities in poverty reduction and sustainable development, in particular in developing countries.	30 full and associate members, including national governments, multilateral institutions, local governments, NGOs, private sector entities
Cities for Mobility (www.cities-for-mobility.net)	To search for policies and concrete measures towards sustainable mobility.	663 members in 85 countries
CLGF - Commonwealth Local Government Forum (www.clgf.org.uk)	To promote and strengthen democratic local government across the Commonwealth	200 members in most of the 53 Countries of the Commonwealth
Global Parliament of Mayors (https://globalparliamentofmayors.org)	A governance body of, by and for mayors from all continents to tackle local challenges resulting from global problems.	60+ mayors

[11] We have not included city networks at the national level. Although there are more national-level networks of cities by far, they are not the focus of this book, which is dedicated to the international outreach of cities.

City network	Scope	Number of members (as of 2018)
ICLEI - Local Governments for Sustainability (www.iclei.org)	To build sustainable futures	1500+ cities, towns and regions
ICORN – International Cities of Refuge Network (www.icorn.org)	To offer long-term temporary refuge to persecuted writers and artists.	+60 cities
METROPOLIS (www.metropolis.org)	Metropolitan governance	139 metropolises
nrg4SD - Network of Regional Governments for Sustainable Development (www.nrg4sd.org)	Climate change, biodiversity and sustainable development	50+ members (states, regions and provinces) from 30 countries on 4 continents
OICC - Organization of Islamic Capitals and Cities (www.oicc.org)	Sustainable development of human settlements	141 capitals and cities as active members, from 54 countries members
R20 – Regions of Climate Action (https://regions20.org)	To support sub-national governments around the world to develop and finance green infrastructure projects	As of 2016, 49 direct members (both national & sub-national authorities), 134 businesses and project facilitators, and 41 investors and financial institutions
Sister Cities International (https://sistercities.org)	To create and strengthen partnerships between communities in the United States and those in other countries and "to promote peace through mutual respect, understanding, and cooperation"	Over 2,000 cities, states and counties partnered in more than 140 countries around the globe.
Strong Cities Network (SCN) (strongcitiesnetwork.org)	Global network to build social cohesion and community resilience to counter violent extremism in all its forms and polarisation.	+120 cities
UCCI - Unión de Ciudades Capitales Iberoamericanas (http://ciudadesiberoamericanas.org)	Cooperation between Ibero-American cities	30 Ibero-American cities (capitals and other major cities of the Americas, Andorra, Portugal and Spain)

City network	Scope	Number of members (as of 2018)
UCLG - United Cities and Local Governments (www.uclg.org)	To represent and defend the interests of local governments on the world stage	+240 towns, cities, regions and metropolises
UN Global Compact Cities Programme (citiesprogramme.org)	A platform for partnered sustainable urban development action	113 cities and regions
World Cities Culture Forum (WCCF) (www.worldcitiescultureforum.com)	To explore the vital role of culture in cities' prosperity.	32 cities
World Mayors Council on Climate Change (www.worldmayorscouncil.org)	Local government leaders to fight climate change	Over 80 members form the World Mayors Council (i.e. Mayors, Former Mayors, Governors and Councillors)

Source: Own elaboration.

Table 7B. **A Selection of City Networks at the Regional Level**

City network	Scope	Number of members (as of 2018)
AEBR - Association of European border regions (www.aebr.eu)	Cross-border cooperation in Europe	Some 100 border and cross-border regions
Arab Towns Organization (ATO) (www.arabtowns.org)	The organization's goal is to preserve the Arab identity of the city and its heritage, including the development and modernization of municipal and local institutions in Arab cities, and the sharing of experiences and cooperation.	20+ Arab cities

City network	Scope	Number of members (as of 2018)
CEMR-CCRE - Council of European Municipalities and Regions (www.ccre.org)	CEMR's work focuses on five thematic areas: governance; environment and climate change; international cooperation; economic, social and territorial cohesion; local and regional public services management	130,000 local and regional authorities united within CEMR's 60 member associations
CityNet (https://citynet-ap.org/)	Regional Network of Local Authorities in the Asia Pacific region to establish more sustainable and resilient cities.	135+ municipalities, NGOs, private companies and research centers.
EFUS – European Forum for Urban Security (https://efus.eu)	European network of local and regional authorities dedicated to urban security	Around 250 local and regional authorities from 16 countries.
Energy Cities (www.energy-cities.eu)	European Association of local authorities in energy transition	More than 1,000 towns and cities in 30 European countries.
Eurocities (www.eurocities.eu)	Network of major European cities that work in different thematic forums (e.g. culture, economy, environment, knowledge society, mobility, social affairs, etc.)	Over 140 of Europe's largest cities and over 45 partner cities.
FLACMA - Federación Latinoamericana de Ciudades, Municipios y Asociaciones de Gobiernos Locales (www.flacma.lat)	To support the consolidation of the agendas of the municipalities and associations of local governments of the region in the different areas that affect local development.	+14 thousand cities and local governments in 22 countries of LATAM and Caribbean
Kitakyushu Initiative for a Clean Environment (KIN) (kitakyushu.iges.or.jp/)	To promote urban environmental actions at the local level in the Asia Pacific region.	62 cities coming from 18 countries in Asia and the Pacific region.

City network	Scope	Number of members (as of 2018)
MedCities (www.medcities.org)	To empower Mediterranean local governments to achieve their strategic priorities	50+ local authorities from all shores of the Mediterranean
MERCOCIUDADES (www.mercociudades.org)	Network of cities in Mercosur to promote their integration and to stimulate development and cooperation between them.	340+ cities in 10 countries in the region
POLIS - European Cities and regions networking for innovate transport solutions (www.polisnetwork.eu)	Sustainable transportation in Europe	70+ cities and regions in Europe
Union of Baltic Cities (UBC) (www.ubc.net)	Leading network of cities in the Baltic Sea Region working in 7 themes: Culture, Inclusion and Health, Planning Cities, Safe Cities, Smart and Prospering Cities, Sustainability, and Youth.	Around 100 Member Cities from Denmark, Estonia, Finland, Germany, Latvia, Lithuania, Norway, Poland, Russia and Sweden

Source: Own elaboration.

International city networks can be an important tool for city governments with common challenges and objectives for sharing ideas and aligning goals and strategies to overcome those challenges. As previously mentioned, city networks vary greatly in terms of size, the issues they deal with, and the goals they have. Still, we can observe three common objectives in most of today's international and regional city networks and associations. These common goals are: (i) to increase cities' voice in the international arena, so as to influence the global decision-making and policy agenda; (ii) to foster peer-learning and exchange information, knowledge, experiences and best practices; and (iii) to connect leaders to discuss shared challenges and settle common goals, and thus accelerating change independently of national governments.

Cities Engaging in the Global Agenda

The proliferation of global city networks in the past decades reveals a clear sign that **cities are increasingly a relevant actor in global governance**. This active involvement has become more evident with the inclusion of cities and urban areas in the rhetoric of the so-called "global agendas." "Global agendas" or "international agendas" consist of those global issues that nation states consider need a special attention; nations then establish a framework for working on those issues. **Two of the most important global agendas today, the United Nations' Sustainable Development Goals (SDGs) and the New Urban Agenda, recognize cities as important actors in defining and implementing policies and initiatives to overcome global challenges.**

UN Member States established the **17 Sustainable Development Goals (SDGs),** also known as the 2030 Agenda for Sustainable Development, in September 2015. The Agenda defines the priorities for development for the next 15 years in 17 goals and 169 global targets (Figure 7).

Figure 7: Sustainable Development Goals (SDGs)

Source: Sustainable Development Knowledge Platform, United Nations.

For the first time, there is a stand-alone goal for cities, *Goal 11: "Make cities and human settlements inclusive, safe, resilient and sustainable."* The goal is narrowed down to a number of targets and indicators related to affordable housing and slum upgrading, access to transport systems, air quality and waste management, and the protection of cultural and natural heritage, among other areas. SDG 11 is important for a number of reasons. First, it is the only "actor-specific" SDG among all the goals. Second, it explicitly recognizes that cities and urbanization are at the forefront of international development, and that urbanization is viewed as something more than just a demographic trend. Cities are acknowledged as key actors in global development and global governance.

Moreover, cities are not just autonomous actors within the context of the SDGs; they are also key contributors to other goals on the sustainable agenda. Due to the numerous connections between cities and the other SDGs, urban areas can be considered the cords that connect virtually all of the SDGs. From "Responsible Consumption and Production" (SDG 12), to "Clean Water and Sanitation" (SDG 6), "Climate Action" (SDG 13), "Reduced Inequalities" (SDG 10), or "Industry, Innovation and Infrastructure" (SDG 9), actions and policies designed and implemented at the local level will have a direct impact on the achievement of many of these sustainable goals.

Lastly, although Member States are the prime actors responsible for tracking and monitoring the progress towards achieving the SDGs, subnational and local governments are also having an important role. It is estimated that 23 percent of all SDGs indicators have a local or urban component that can be measured at the local level (City Prosperity Initiative, n.d.). Therefore, sub-national and local governments have key roles not only in implementing the right urban policies to achieve the targets, but also in following up and monitoring progress to advance the urban agenda.

In addition, the Third Conference on Housing and Sustainable Urban Development, also known as **Habitat III**, defined the **New Urban Agenda** (NUA). The NUA – adopted in October 2016 in Quito - establishes a new framework for the role of cities and urban policies at different levels of governance. It emphasizes the role of subnational and local governments in the implementation and localization of policies, and the importance of partnerships to overcome global challenges and to achieve the SDGs. Therefore, the NUA complements and reinforces the urban-related dimensions of the SDGS, by defining approaches on how to plan, design and manage cities that are sustainable and in line with the SDGs.

As these two important global agendas clearly recognize, **cities are well positioned to take the lead in addressing global challenges**. From developing more sustainable patterns of production and consumption, to planning more sustainable and affordable housing, to developing safer and more efficient urban transportation systems, cities have the capabilities, resources, and enabling factors such as policies and regulations, to find solutions to the world's most critical challenges and help populations shift toward sustainable development.

***

2.5 Perils of Global Cities

As we have seen throughout the different book volumes of this series, urbanization processes frequently bring about economic growth, progress and rising living standards. Productivity tends to be substantially greater in cities than in rural areas. Richard Florida developed an *urban productivity ratio* to compare the economic output of metropolitan areas to the per capita economic output of their nations as a whole. The ratio indicates that "the typical large metro in the United States or Europe or Japan has an urban productivity ratio of 1 to 1.25, indicating productivity on par or perhaps 25 percent greater than the national average" (Florida, 2014). This suggests that urbanization is indeed a force for economic development and economic growth.

However, urban areas are also hubs of inequality, segregation and poverty. **Large cities tend to be more unequal than the countries that host them**. For instance, income inequality in the New York Metropolitan Area (MSA) is significantly higher than the U.S. average (Behrens and Robert-Nicoud, 2014). Moreover, **growing processes of exclusion, segregation and gentrification are increasingly critical challenges in cities** in general (see *Cities and Social Cohesion* (Berrone, Ricart, and Duch, 2017)), and in global cities in particular. In the developed world, cities are becoming more spatially segregated as gentrification or urban regeneration increasingly push people out of city centers. This is happening in cities such as New York, London, Paris, San Francisco and Berlin.

Moreover, global cities tend to be more innovative as they are the nodes of global connectivity and information flows. In a recent study analyzing the impact of the rise of knowledge-based activities on spatial inequality and segregation within U.S. cities, it was found "that innovation intensity was responsible for 20% of the overall increase in urban segregation between 1990 and 2010" (Berkes and Gaetani, 2018). The main reason for this effect was the clustering of employment and place of workers working in innovative and knowledge-based industries. The San Francisco Bay Area and Silicon Valley is a well-known example. On one hand, Silicon Valley is a global center for high technology and innovation. On the other hand, San Francisco Metropolitan Area has a high level of income inequality, with families on the top 5 percent of households in the metropolitan area earning incomes 11 times as high as the bottom 20 percent of households in 2016 (Berube, 2018). As Florida mentions, "the very same clustering forces that generates economic and social progress also divides us" (Florida, 2017).

This is one of the paradoxes in many global innovative cities: as cities become more global, innovative and economically powerful, they can also become more segregated and unequal.

Furthermore, in the developing world, the lack of affordable housing and basic infrastructures in urban areas are still of critical importance. Despite significant progress achieved in reducing the proportion of people living in slums around the world, which has been decreasing in recent years, the total number of individuals living in slums or informal settlements has actually increased from 807 to 883 million from 2000 to 2014 (UN-Habitat, 2018), due to population growth. **Developing countries are urbanizing rapidly and the proliferation of slums is still a perilous issue, in particular in Sub-Saharan Africa.** In fact, the highest levels of income inequality are generally located in cities in either Sub-Saharan Africa or the Americas.

Table 8 shows socio-economic indicators of a selected group of global cities. On one hand, we have included "traditional" global cities of the "Global North," such as New York, Tokyo, London and Paris. On the other hand, we have included the up-and-coming global cities of the Global South, such as Mexico City, Sao Paolo, Shenzhen and Bangkok.

Table 8. Some Socio-economic Indicators for Selected Traditional and Rising Global Cities, 2017

Metropolitan City	Population	GDP at PPP (Million international $)	GINI index	Unemployment (%)	Productivity (US$ p. p. employed in constant prices)	Real GDP growth (% growth)
Tokyo (Japan)	37,264,500	1,818,041	34.8	3.1	81,316.8	3.6
New York (USA)	20,170,500	1,739,653	49.5	4.5	169,674.1	1.6

Metropolitan City	Population	GDP at PPP (Million international $)	GINI index	Unemployment (%)	Productivity (US$ p. p. employed in constant prices)	Real GDP growth (% growth)
Los Angeles (USA)	13,344,700	1,056,144	50.1	4.9	155,394.6	1.3
Moscow (Russia)	19,929,800	1,052,105	43.2	2.2	32,284.2	2.2
London (UK)	16,304,500	1,036,275	35.0	4.9	97,544.6	3.4
Seoul (South Korea)	25,392,700	1,010,454	35.1	4.2	51,655.9	1.9
Paris (France)	11,827,300	852,140	38.0	8.9	131,434.3	2.6
Shanghai (China)	25,029,200	841,618	47.2	4.1	32,100.8	2.1
Beijing (China)	22,778,400	770,897	37.3	1.5	33,237.6	1.7
Jakarta (Indonesia)	31,509,400	763,582	45.5	7.8	16,011.9	5.2
Chicago (USA)	9,551,500	681,510	46.9	5.2	136,540.2	6.3
Bangkok (Thailand)	17,264,800	643,254	41.4	1.0	22,485.5	5.8
Shenzhen (China)	11,762,200	585,993	44.5	2.3	33,425.0	0.9
Mexico City (Mexico)	21,316,700	584,252	45.9	5.0	28,049.3	5.4
Washington (USA)	6,194,200	537,004	42.9	3.6	155,904.5	-0.5
Singapore (Singapore)	5,612,300	527,129	45.9	2.2	84,642.0	1.6
São Paulo (Brazil)	21,530,200	513,776	55.1	14.7	23,226.6	1.7
San Francisco (USA)	4,534,400	498,543	46.1	3.6	188,802.3	8.0
Hong Kong (China)	7,391,700	454,866	52.5	3.1	85,326.1	2.3
Buenos Aires (Argentina)	14,245,800	388,530	38.7	8.8	41,242.2	-2.4
Delhi (India)	17,693,100	359,896	38.9	4.2	14,627.6	2.8

Chapter 2: Trends and Challenges of Cities

Metropolitan City	Population	GDP at PPP (Million international $)	GINI index	Unemployment (%)	Productivity (US$ p. p. employed in constant prices)	Real GDP growth (% growth)
Mumbai (India)	19,044,200	355,642	28.3	3.0	12,504.1	-0.4
Madrid (Spain)	6,459,500	336,487	42.5	14.0	79,044.0	2.8
Kuala Lumpur (Malaysia)	7,546,800	335,409	49.5	3.0	28,778.9	3.3
Toronto (Canada)	6,262,100	285,732	42.7	6.6	76,784.8	3.0
Sydney (Australia)	4,941,700	285,643	40.9	4.9	115,497.8	6.1
Rio de Janeiro (Brazil)	13,000,500	254,283	56.0	12.2	23,149.8	1.9
Barcelona (Spain)	5,488,600	250,096	35.2	12.3	69,264.2	3.4
Dubai (UAE)	5,408,900	247,458	45.5	2.8	33,864.0	7.4
Berlin (Germany)	5,208,400	230,235	32.0	5.5	71,988.5	0.7
Melbourne (Australia)	4,601,700	225,659	40.3	6.5	95,850.0	6.9
Santiago (Chile)	7,411,400	210,793	39.2	7.2	35,192.5	1.5
Lima (Peru)	10,232,100	199,807	40.3	9.3	19,500.1	3.3
Tel Aviv (Israel)	3,913,900	180,884	36.0	3.9	89,676.9	0.3
Brussels (Belgium)	2,732,500	167,955	39.1	9.8	122,378.9	1.0
Vienna (Austria)	3,066,200	162,063	39.4	8.0	96,755.1	3.3
Amsterdam (Netherlands)	1,507,900	140,854	37.7	5.5	143,910.5	1.0

Metropolitan City	Population	GDP at PPP (Million international $)	GINI index	Unemployment (%)	Productivity (US$ p. p. employed in constant prices)	Real GDP growth (% growth)
Lagos (Nigeria)	10,773,600	116,382	64.4	7.7	9,092.0	3.6
Johannesburg (South Africa)	5,076,900	102,632	63.2	28.7	21,011.0	3.8

Source: Own elaboration based on data from Euromonitor International.

Note: Total Population: Euromonitor International from national statistics/UN

GDP Measured at Purchasing Power Parity: Euromonitor International from national statistics/Eurostat/OECD/UN/International Monetary Fund (IMF), International Financial Statistics (IFS)

Gini Index: Euromonitor International from national statistics.

Unemployment Rate: Euromonitor International from International Labour Organisation (ILO)/Eurostat/national statistics/OECD.

Productivity: Euromonitor International from International Labour Organisation (ILO)/Eurostat/national statistics.

Real GDP Growth: Euromonitor International from national statistics/Eurostat/OECD/UN/International Monetary Fund (IMF), World Economic Outlook (WEO).

In order to take advantage of the opportunities offered by increasing urbanization and globalization, while reducing the negative effects of larger populations (poverty, inequality, segregation, increasing pressure to use limited resources, etc.), local governments and **city managers around the world need to plan and invest strategically**. First, they need to design and implement strategies that will allow cities to take advantage of their global connectivity and spur overall economic growth, while making sure that the resulting economic growth will not only impact a small part of the society and result in higher inequalities and gaps. Second, they need to invest in all kinds of infrastructures (water systems, mass transport, digital infrastructure, affordable housing, etc.) that will allow for prosperity and development. This is of key importance for cities both in the developing world and in the developed world.

How city leaders and local policymakers respond to the problems and challenges of global cities in the 21st century will determine if we succeed or fail in the creation of more sustainable, prosperous and inclusive urban hubs. Section 3 will analyze some case studies and best practices that provide solutions and strategies that cities around the world have implemented or are implementing. These strategies take full advantage of global networks, with the aim of increasing prosperity and improve the quality of life of cities' citizens.

***

3. Best Practices and Case Studies of Global Cities

From ancient trading cities to modern networked global cities, urban areas tend to take advantage of international opportunities. With increasing urbanization and technology-driven globalization, cities are acquiring a new role in the global economy and in the international arena as they enjoy a key central position in today's globalized and interconnected world. To take advantage of their centrality and with the final aim of promoting themselves abroad in order to attract visitors, events, foreign investment, students, etc., and to encourage cultural, political and economic exchanges, **cities carry out many different activities and strategies in order to increase their "attractiveness," international visibility and recognition**.

If cities want to attract resources, mitigate the negative consequences of rising global competition and continue being hubs of international networks of exchange, they need to address such opportunities and challenges with actions and solutions. **Urban managers need to design and implement global strategies, policies and plans to reap the benefits brought by increased connectivity, while dealing with the negative effects of a globalized economy and society**. The capacity to act in a coordinated manner, both internally and in collaboration with the private sector, will be crucial for a city's international strategy to succeed.

Some cities have explicitly established outward-looking strategies, such as the setting up of specific agencies for internationalization or the creation of specific programs or initiatives to improve the image and global presence of their cities. While there is no single model or strategy for global action in cities, urban leaders and city managers can look at the experiences of other cities in defining initiatives, measures or plans to improve the city's openness, to tackle the potential negative consequences of globalization, and/or to leverage its position in the international arena.

In this section, we will examine some best practices, experiences and case studies of cities around the world regarding the international dimension of cities. As in the previous book volumes of this series, we will make use of **the Smart Urban Management Model (SUMM) as a framework of analysis**. In the SUMM, we have defined five levers of change or dimensions of action that can help city managers and urban planners identify solutions and articulate initiatives and practices to overcome urban challenges. In this case, these are related to the internationalization of cities. Figure 8 presents the overall framework of analysis.

Figure 8. Smart urban management model

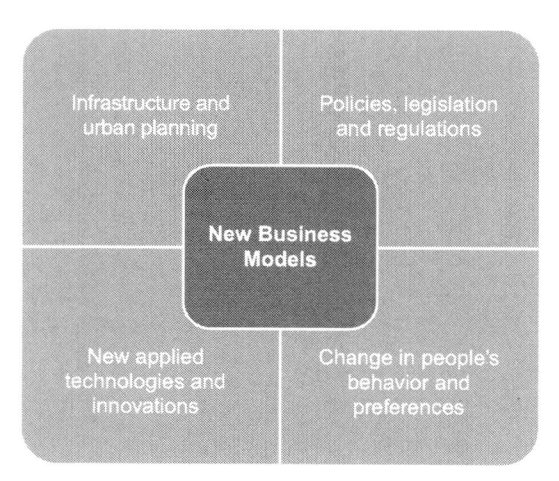

Source: Prepared by the authors.

Rising globalization exacerbates many of the challenges of cities in the 21st century. However, it also offers huge opportunities. Implementing the right policies, legislation and regulations will be crucial for cities to take advantage of their new central role in the global economy and have a greater voice and influence in global governance. For instance, adjusting regulatory frameworks to be more appealing to international markets and to facilitate international trade or FDI attraction, or adjusting policies to attract and retain international talent can be key tools for globalizing cities.

Second, in order to design cities that are open to the world in this age of globalization, improving a city's connectedness and infrastructures, both hard and soft, is of critical importance. First, improving a city's built infrastructure, such as the water and sewage system, and transportation connectivity, including airports, ports, road and railway system, enhances international mobility, transportation and logistics. Second, in order to continue being relevant in today's service and information economy, cities must develop quality ICT infrastructure and telecommunication networks that facilitate accessibility to technology and information.

In this regard, new technologies and innovations can offer huge opportunities to improve connectivity and the development of new business models. The digital revolution has eliminated national borders and facilitated exchanges of all kinds directly among local levels. The democratization of information has facilitated accessibility, communication and engagement. This has brought challenges and opportunities in equal measure. On one hand, ICTs have allowed for new forms of citizen engagement and decision making to develop. They have also established new spaces for collaboration. On the other hand, ICTs have the potential for creating new dynamics of inclusion and exclusion. Attending issues of the "digital divide" is of critical importance for city managers. The challenge for local policymakers is to make use of the opportunities offered by new applied technologies and innovation, but at the same time ensure participation and inclusion in a more democratic way.

Changes in technology, along with greater communication and connectivity worldwide, have triggered changes in people's behavior, preferences and concerns. City leaders should take into account social preferences and behavioral changes, when designing and implementing policies related to the international outreach of cities. For instance, in the tourism industry, changes in consumer habits and the development of new technologies have facilitated greater interaction among local governments, tourists and city dwellers. As a result, co-created travel experiences are now possible, which take into account the preferences and concerns of all the stakeholders involved.

Therefore, as cities increasingly take on the role of global players, it is in their best interest to engage with stakeholders, take advantage of the opportunities offered by globalization and remain relevant in the new international order. In this section, some of the strategies and tools for the internationalization of cities will be highlighted.

***

3.1. Global Strategy and International Promotion

Due to their starring role in the global economy, as hubs of information and global communications flows and central points in the flow of people, cities are amassing growing power and influence at the global level. In order to take advantage of the opportunities offered by the changing international system and respond to the resulting pressures and challenges, it is in cities' best interest to promote their local interests in the world and to position themselves more effectively within the international sphere.

In order to do so, **city governments have incentives to internationalize and/or to define a global strategy in order to unleash the city's external**

potential. From setting up specific agencies for city internationalization, to defining a more comprehensive global strategy for the city, to specific urban marketing campaigns, cities are increasingly implementing outward-looking strategies. International promotion at the city level is crucial for two main reasons that reinforce each other. One key reason is that the attraction of foreign investment, trade, tourism and international talent and workforce at the city level has the potential to contribute to the local economy and to increase competitiveness in the global market. The second reason is that, in a context of fierce competition, a defined global strategy can contribute to enhancing the city's image and reputation, and clearly differentiating itself at the international level from other cities.

Many cities around the world have set up **international promotion agencies**. Some of these agencies are focused on a specific area, such as trade promotion and investment attraction offices or the tourism promotion agencies, as we will discuss later, while others gather a combination of all of these in a single agency. When there are different agencies, these need to be coordinated, following a single common global strategy.

International promotion offices at the city level can be public, private or public-private partnerships (PPP). For instance, a case of a publicly created international city agency would be the International Promotion Office of the Madrid City Council, created in 2015 to coordinate the promotion of the city of Madrid at the international level.[12] There are also examples of private initiatives, such as the Barcelona Global initiative, a private, independent association of companies, research centers, entrepreneurs, business schools, universities and cultural institutions to attract and retain talent and economic activity (Barcelona Global, n.d.). Finally, we can also find city promotional agencies formed as a PPP, as in the case of the London's promotional agency London & Partners. (See Box 3.)

---

[12] See Madrid for you: http://www.madridforyou.es/en

BOX 3. London & Partners

London & Partners, the Mayor of London's official promotional agency, was established in 2011 as a PPP to strength the local economy, improve the city's reputation, and promote the city of London as a world city in which to invest, work, study and visit (London & Partners, n.d.). It was created by merging three previous agencies, Visit London, Think London and Study London, which focused on attracting visitors, businesses and students respectively.

Today, the agency work in different areas such as:

- International Business: attracting FDI and help London companies grow
- Boosting leisure and business tourism in the city
- Attracting and promoting major sporting, entertainment and cultural events
- Promoting London to international students
- Work on London's brand

London, UK.

In the period 2016-2017, the agency contributed to adding £340m to London's economy, created or supported 10,112 jobs, set up or expanded close to 300 overseas companies, attracted 854 events, and helped create 19,175 positive articles in international media (London & Partners, 2017).

As part of this positive image or brand creation, in 2016, following the Brexit referendum, the Mayor of London Sadiq Khan started the **#LondonIsOpen** campaign to show that London was still open to business, visitors and students. London & Partners supported and promoted the campaign, including a weeklong program of trade missions to Berlin, Paris and Madrid to ensure trade and investment (London & Partners, 2017).

This is a good example of a common agency coordinating all promotion activities of a city, including attraction of business, tourists and students, as well as improving the international image and reputation of a city.

Moreover, some cities have also attempted to create **a more comprehensive global strategy for their cities**. For instance, the city of Bristol (UK), has defined a 10-year international strategy (2017-2027), called "Bristol: Global City," which aims not only to attract trade and investment, but also to promote global values such as human rights, inclusivity and sustainability. It also seeks to take advantage of the city's diversity as a source for creativity, innovation and dynamism (Bristol City Council, 2018). Another example is the city of Guangzhou (China), which has defined the aim of becoming a global city as part of its Master Plan 2035, leveraging its history as an international trade hub. (See Box 4.)

Policies, legislation and regulations

BOX 4. Guangzhou Global City

For almost 2,000 years, since the Qin Dynasty, Guangzhou has been a center of trade between Chinese and foreigners, while serving as China's "maritime gateway" to other parts of Asia, the Middle East and southern Europe. In the 14th century, the first Ming emperor forbade all private Chinese international trade, restraining Guangzhou's trading role; but the port city recovered its key role in international maritime trade with European merchants in the 17th and 18th centuries, (Mathews, Lin, and Yang, 2017). In the 19th century, during the so-called Opium Wars, Guangzhou became controlled by European powers, and after that its role as center of foreignness was reduced. It was not until the end of the 20th century, that Guangzhou, also known as Canton, actively re-emerged as a global city. But Guangzhou's role as an international city is not new.

In past decades, with the Chinese Open Door Policy and the rise of the Pearl River Delta region (one of the largest urban agglomerations on the planet, including big cities such as Guangzhou, Shenzhen, Macau, Hong Kong, Foshan and Dongguan, and a major factory for the world), Guangzhou has increased exponentially in size and influence. The city has experienced an accelerated urbanization process, moving from a population of around 1 million people in 1950 to some 14 million inhabitants in 2018 – and it is expected to continue growing to 20 million people by 2035. Its economy has also expanded extraordinarily with an average annual growth rate of 13% over the past decade, reaching a GDP of more than US$300 billion in 2017 (2,150.32 RMB billion) (HKTDC, 2018).

As a major trading port, Guangzhou's 2017 exports accounted for 13.7% of all of Guangdong Province's exports. The Canton Fair (China Import and Export Fair) is the largest trade fair in the world. In 2017 Guangzhou received 62.75 million overnight visitors, with 3.46 million of them being international (HKTDC, 2018), and was ranked 5th as a Chinese top destination for overseas tourists. In our Cities in Motion Index 2019, the city of Guangzhou ranked #90 in the international outreach dimension, the 4th Chinese city in this dimension only after Hong Kong, Beijing and Shanghai (Berrone, Ricart, Duch and Carrasco, 2019). (See Appendix II).

> Thus, the international dimension of the city is already quite strong. In its quest to become an international city, the City of Guangzhou released the "Guangzhou Master Plan from 2017 to 2035," which sets a vision for becoming a dynamic and vibrant global city by 2035. The Master Plan aims at becoming an international transportation hub, a trade center, a scientific and technological industry innovation hub, or to expand international communications, among other targets. The final aim is to continue promoting the construction of Guangzhou as a global city.

Lastly, there are also examples of cities' global strategies emerging from a civil society organization, rather than a city government. For instance, the Chicago Council on Global Affairs – an independent, nonpartisan organization and think tank that aims to provide insights on critical global issues – has attempted to create a comprehensive global strategy, the so-called "Chicago's Global Strategy" roadmap. This global strategy was developed in coordination with all the stakeholders of the City of Chicago with the goal of advancing the city in this direction (Chicago Council on Global Affairs, 2017).

These are just a few examples of cities in different parts of the world trying to strengthen their international promotion policies and define global strategies. The next section will focus on how cities seek to enhance their images, brands and reputations.

3.1.1. City Image, Brand and Reputation

Many places are often connected to specific images and ideas. For instance, the collective imagery that relates Paris with romance and love has developed gradually over the decades. Another example is the city of Rome, also known "the Eternal City," which is well-known for its magnificent history and arts. However, as competition between cities accelerates, managers and planners of many urban hubs around the world increasingly want to build positive images for their cities.

Slogan of New York City

The creation and growth of a city's image or identity can occur gradually and naturally – as in the previous two city examples – or it can be created artificially. For example, municipalities around the world are building architecturally stunning buildings to create images that are easily recognized, such as the Sydney Opera House in Sydney, or the Burj Khalifa in Dubai – the world's tallest building since 2009. In addition, urban managers are also designing specific public relations campaigns to promote the city, such as slogans or logos. One of the best-known examples is the "I ♥ NY" slogan of the city of New York, created in the 1970s as part of an advertising campaign to promote tourism in the state of New York.

All of these marketing initiatives or promotion strategies are part of what is usually called **city branding, city marketing**, or simply, **city promotion**. Techniques for creating a city brand identity often include many of the abovementioned strategies, such as using symbols (e.g. landmarks and monuments) and visual slogans or logos; as well as developing a reputation related to culture, arts or sports, among other areas. These marketing tactics aim to produce a positive image for the city in order to attract the highest possible value from global flows (economic and financial flows; labor flows; information flows, etc.) to promote local development, improve the city's competitiveness and, increase welfare and prosperity (Anttiroiko, 2015). They also aspire to create a "unique city identity" that is easily recognizable so that residents, visitors, businesses and investors from all over the world can connect with the municipality (Oguztimur and Akturan, 2016). However, building an identity to the extent that it creates its own brand is a difficult task, since it usually demands a clear vision and strategic management.

Mayors and city planners worldwide are becoming increasingly more aware of the critical importance of their cities' image, since it affects multiple issues. First, a positive city image can boost trade, investment and business transactions. Second, it can be also critical in tourists' choice to decide where to go. Lastly, a good city image can also enhance the attraction and retention of talent. **As the global competition between cities on the international scale intensifies, the successful development of attraction-oriented, city branding and urban marketing strategies is becoming more important than ever.**

Accordingly, city leaders are increasingly developing strategic initiatives and specific marketing and branding strategies to promote an attractive image for their cities; develop a city's unique identity and international position; and influence people's perceptions. Although a city's image or reputation is not independent from national perceptions, and some elements of a city's image are external and cannot be controlled by city managers, a city's image can vary significantly from one city to another, with clear distinctions between cities within the same country. As a result, there are some strategies that city leaders can put in place in order to improve the image of their city (See Box 5).

BOX 5. Strategies for Improving a City's Image

A previous study carried out by the authors titled *"What City Has the Best Image?"* (Berrone, Ricart, and Carrasco, 2014), analyzed the media coverage of 20 large cities between 2008 and 2012, as a proxy to assess the image of a city. In general, how a city is represented in the news media influences the general public, both positively and negatively.

On the one hand, positive aspects such as sport events and cultural developments, are often associated with a positive perception and broad awareness of a city. The study found that sports-related news (especially big events) tend to translate to a positive image of the city. These events put the city on a map and can improve domestic and foreign investments. However, hosting a major event is not a guaranteed strategy, since it also entails risky large-scale investments, as well as many uncertainties.

The study mentions other variables, such as human factors and natural factors, that can result in an important negative shock to the city's image. More specifically, crime and terrorism are two of the worst problems for a city's image. Terrorism tends to have a huge effect, but on the short run. For instance, after the terrorist attacks in Paris in January and November 2015, and Nice in July 2016, tourism contracted sharply. However, slightly more than one year later, tourists were returning to Paris again (Euronews, 2017). Crime has a similar negative effect, but it tends to be more in the long term. Additionally, natural disasters, such as hurricanes, floods or earthquakes, also result in a negative effect for the city. For example, the 2004 Indian Ocean earthquake and tsunami – which resulted in more than 200,000 people killed and affected 14 countries – led to a sharp downturn in the tourism industry in many of the affected countries, such as Indonesia and Thailand (Langill, 2015). Yet, after a couple of years, the tourism industry had recovered.

As a result, the study shows that the image of a city is very sensitive to both positive and negative events. The authors identify five key strategies to deal with these positive and negative effects that tend to be largely covered by the media (Berrone et al., 2014):

1. *Encouraging visits to the city,* so people can experience first-hand the reality of the city.

2. *Hosting spotlight events.* Taking into account socio-economic costs, worldwide events can be a good opportunity to improve a city's image.

3. *Solving the problem that led to the negative image.* This is especially true for problems like crime. For instance, in Medellin (Colombia) the sharp decline in crime since the 1980s, and specially the improvement in the past two decades, has resulted in a significant increase in the number of foreign visiting the city, with a 160% growth in the number of visitors from between 2008 and 2017 (SITUR, 2016).

4. *Delivering counter-stereotypical messages.*

5. *Acknowledging the negative image.* Identifying where the weaknesses and the main problems of the city lie is the first step for defining a strategy for solving them.

Furthermore, **a city's image is also about reputation and perception**. The City RepTrak®, prepared by the Reputation Institute, ranks the world's 56 most reputable cities based on levels of trust, esteem, admiration and respect.[13] In 2018, the city with the strongest reputation worldwide according to the City RepTrak® was Tokyo - leading in respected leaders and effective governement - followed by Sydney (#2), Copenhagen (#3), Vienna (#4) and Stockholm (#5) (Reputation Institute, 2018).

Since there is a direct link between a city's reputation and the public's preference to visit, work and live in that city, **it is in the city's best interest to manage their image, brand and reputation if they want to attract visitors, residents, investors and business**. In order to do so, it is important to work together with all relevant stakeholders and to align strategies and initatives for common goals.

BOX 6. Hamburg: Developing a City Brand

Hamburg is the second largest city in Germany after Berlin, with a population of over 1.8 million people. Officially, The Free and Hanseatic City of Hamburg, the city is both a municipality and a city-state within the Federal Republic of Germany. As Europe's third-largest port, Hamburg is an economic, cultural and education hub, as well as a major touristic destination.

Hamburg, Germany.

---

[13] The 2018 City RepTrak® is a global survey based on more than 12,000 ratings, collected in the G8 countries.

Prior to the 2000s, the city of Hamburg didn't have a clear brand. The metropolis had different city marketing bodies targeting different markets that were not clearly coordinated (The Place Brand Observer, 2017). However, in 2004, and after losing against Leipzig in the competition to host the Olympic Games, a conscious process of city brand development and management was launched in the city (Järvisalo, 2012).

Since then, strategic city brand building was declared a top priority for the city. Marketing activities were coordinated among the different partners involved and a unified management for the city brand of Hamburg was designed. In fact, Hamburg was one of the first cities in Germany and in Europe developing an integrated approach to city branding. Since there is a close link between a city brand and the identity, values and elements that characterize that city, in 2004 and 2009 two comprehensive market surveys were carried out to identify the positive perceptions people associated with Hamburg. The survey's results were used to develop the Hamburg brand around 10 (now 12) success modules, such as "Metropolis on the waterfront", "Street festivals and events", "Cultural offer", "Metropolis for living", "Shopping metropolis", "International trading metropolis" or "Attractive business environment" (Hamburg Marketing GmbH, n.d.).

In 2012, the holding Hamburg Marketing was created to integrate all marketing activities of the City of Hamburg into one single entity gathering four entities: The Hamburg Marketing GmbH (HMG), the Hamburg Tourismus GmbH, the Hamburg Convention Bureau and the HWF Hamburg Business Development Corporation (Hamburg Marketing GmbH, n.d.). The company involves all municipal stakeholders and specialized authorities, such as the City of Hamburg, the Hamburg Chamber of Commerce and the Hamburg Metropolitan Region, with the goal to "raise and expand Hamburg's attractiveness".

Source: (Hamburg Marketing GmbH, 2011)

The political initiative to create the Hamburg Marketing holding is a good example of a coordinated brand planning process and implementation.

***

3.2. Trade and Investment

Trade has been a key feature of the internationalization of cities since the first ancient trading cities. Cities and their metropolitan areas have always benefited from having privileged access to global networks of exchange of goods and services. Cities usually possess the physical assets and infrastructures that are essential for international trade, such as seaports and airports, as well as the highest levels of human capital and financial resources. However, national governments have traditionally been the principal regulators in trade and investment. From negotiating trade deals, to establishing tariffs and tax regimes, or providing investment incentives, countries are generally the main actors defining and establishing trade and investment policies.

Yet, as urban areas continue to concentrate population and economic activity, the role of cities as international trading hubs intensifies. As mentioned in our book *Cities and the Economy* (Berrone, Ricart, and Duch T-Figueras, 2017), urban areas already are the nodal points in GVC, forming and concentrating clusters of manufacturing and service activities. With the revolution of ICTs and the diffusion of international production networks, the rules of the game are changing, and cities have the potential to play a more direct and relevant role in regards to attracting and managing international trade and investment.

In order to take advantage of changes in the international trade system, cities and regions around the world are setting specific city agencies for trade promotion and investment attraction. Given their proximity to local businesses and local investors, subnational agencies tend to become experts of their territories, as they best know their business structure and industrial fabric, and can recognize what sectors or activities ideally match local resources and capabilities. As a result, **local trade and investment promotion agencies usually offer more tailored, customer-focused**

options and tend to be more innovative and efficient in matchmaking than national ones. These subnational agencies might be supported by local governments, the private sector or, more often, a combination of public-private-partnerships (PPP) at the local level.

> Policies, legislation and regulations

BEST PRACTICE: MIAMI International Trade Office
— From a tourism-dependent economy to an international business hub

Miami, United States

Source: Pixabay, CC0.

The city of Miami is the seat of the Miami-Dade County, the most populous county in the State of Florida (US) with a population of some 2.7 million people in 34 municipalities (The city of Miami itself has around 400,000 inhabitants). Miami is located in a plain between the Everglades to the west and Biscayne Bay to the east; and it is the cultural, economic and financial center of South Florida. Additionally, the Miami-Fort Lauderdale-West Palm Beach metropolitan area has a combined population of more than 6 million people, ranked seventh largest in the United States (Statista, 2017).

The Miami metro area is a leader in commerce, international trade, arts and entertainments, tourism as well as finance, with the largest concentration of international banks in the US and home to many MNCs headquarters. In 2017, the Miami-Fort Lauderdale-West Palm Beach metro area had a Gross Metropolitan Product of around US$300 billion chained (2009) (Statista, 2017). However, the urban area of Miami is one of the places in the US with the highest level of inequality. For instance, a recent study by GOBankingRates, showed that in the Miami area, the top 1% earns 45 times more than the bottom 99% - being the

3rd most unequal metro area in the United States -, and 20% of the Miami-Dade County's population lives below the poverty rate (GOBankingRates, 2018).

Miami is often referred to as the "Cruise Capital of the World" – due to the millions of passengers going through PortMiami every year -, and as the "Cargo Gateway of the Americas" - due to its central role as global leading hub for global commerce, especially as a key port of entry for cargo from South America and the Caribbean. Therefore, both the tourism industry and the international business industry are key sectors for the Miami's economy.

Context

- For most of Miami's history, and up to the end of the 20th century, the city's economy has been primarily based on tourism.
- Miami has important geographical and cultural connections with Latin America and Europe. The city is located close to the Latin America and the Caribbean markets, and it has received large numbers of Latin America's migrants since the 1960s.
- Miami has traditionally had a very diverse population. In 2000, around half of the Miami-Dade County population was foreign-born, with the vast majority of them having a Latin America's origin (Miami-Dade County, 2009).

Actions

- Building on its success as a tourism destination and its well-established connections with the rest of the world geographically and culturally, in particular with Latin America, the city of Miami looked for a way to use these advantages and capture the increasingly growing Latin American and Caribbean and European markets.
- In 2002, the Jay Malina International Trade Consortium (ITC) was created as a county government agency to promote and strengthen international trade in the Miami-Dade County (Haar, 2008). The ITC advises on issues related to the Miami-Dade County's international trade agenda, establishes program priorities, recommends the agency's budget, etc.
- The International Trade Promotion Unit established the goal of promoting international trade and positioning Miami-Dade County as a global hub of international trade. It provides a number of services such as offering access to financial services, helping local companies access global markets, and several training services for staff in international trade issues. In other words, it offers financial support, coordination and certification to outgoing trade missions

(Haar, 2008). In order to facilitate information, the ITC has a web page[14], where information on international trade and business activities can be found, as well as on the Sister Cities Program, international missions and a list of international trade offices and consulates.

- Additionally, Miami-Dade Beacon Council, a public-private partnership constituting the Miami-Dade County's Official Economic Development Office founded in 1985, has been a very important actor recruiting, expanding and retaining businesses, as well as attracting foreign direct investments. In 2016, Florida received US$10.5 billion in FDI, which represents approximately 2.8% of the U.S total (Florida Chamber of Commerce, 2017).

- Moreover, although Miami is not in a top position in the U.S. urban hierarchy, the City and the ITC have done a lot of work in order to attract international institutions. The Miami area is home to over 100 foreign consulates, foreign trade offices and bi-national chambers of commerce, which helps increasing and establishing the city's global role.

Miami, United States

Source: Pixabay, CC0.

Outcomes

- Over the past decades, Miami has managed to move away from a tourist-dependent economy, into being an important international trading and business hub, with a more diversified economy.

- This has resulted from a number of initiatives and strategies to take advantage of the city's unique factors, such as its geography and diverse populations, and turn these factors into the city's strengths to diversify the economy and open up to the world.

---

[14] See: http://www.miamidade.gov/business/international-trade.asp.

- Today, Miami's economy is highly diversified, with strong industries including tourism, trade, real estate and finance, as well as creative and health industries.
- Additionally, the City has implemented a number of strategies to build a strong brand and to enhance the city's reputation as an open and global city. In fact, the city is known as the "Gateway to the Americas" or "Gateway to Latin America," due to its role as a center of international trade with those areas. Overall, about one-third of all U.S. exports to Latin America flows through the Miami metropolitan area.
- Today, international trade plays an important role in the economy of Miami-Dade County, supporting over 100,000 jobs and being one of the key industries in the County. Miami Customs District #52 (South Florida's) total stock with the rest of the world has increased from US$65.9 billion in 2012 to US$107 billion in 2017 (Miami-Dade County, 2018a). Additionally, the trade surplus of the Miami District #52 amounted to US$10.6 billion in 2017, remaining one of a very few U.S. Customs Districts that continues to enjoy a trade surplus (Ibid.).
- Miami's International Airport and the Port of Miami are two important international trade infrastructures. Miami International Airport is the largest international cargo gateway in the United States and 11th busiest globally, with 2.2 million tons of cargo annually (MIA, 2019). Additionally, the Port of Miami is the second largest economic engine in Miami-Dade County, contributing US$41.4 billion annually to the local economy and supporting more than 324,352 jobs in South Florida (Miami-Dade County, 2018b).
- Additionally, according to the WorldCity's research, all 10 of the world's largest logistics firms have offices in South Florida, and some 1,400 multinationals are based on the area (Roberts, 2016).
- According to the Globalization and World Cities Research Network (GaWC), a renowned think tank that studies world cities, Miami is considered an alpha-city, which refers to "a very important world city that links major economic regions and states into the world economy" (GaWC, 2018a).
- Lastly, in the 2015-2017 Strategic Plan of the City of Miami it is stated that the city's strategic vision is to be "an internationally-renowned city with a commitment to public engagement and excellent service delivery; a diverse and vibrant community with a high quality of life; and a global destination for business, culture, and leisure" (The City of Miami, 2016). This exhibits a clear outward-looking strategy from the City of Miami.

Besides international trade promotion, cities and regions are also increasingly institutionalizing investment attraction. The growing importance of investment promotion as a global business and the creation of **Investment Promotion Agencies (IPAs)** is a relatively new phenomenon that has expanded rapidly since the 1980s and the 1990s (UN, 2001). Governments, first at the national level, but more recently also at the local level, are recognizing the critical role of attracting and facilitating investments to economic growth and development – both as a source of finance and as a tool to acquire and develop expertise and knowledge. As a result, governments around the world have stepped up the creation of investment promotion organizational structures.

At the city level, local governments are more vigorously promoting their respective regions to foreign investors. For instance, the World Association of Investment Promotion Agencies (WAIPA) – which gathers investment promotion agencies around the world – has 170 members, over one-third of them agencies from cities or regions (Tavares-Lehmann and Tavares, 2017). This is an example of how cities are gradually designing policies and implementing institutions to attract increased flows of FDI. As in the case of trade promotion agencies, subnational IPAs can be the result of a government-led initiative, directly through private investors, or some kind of PPP.

Chapter 3: Best Practices and Case Studies of Global Cities

>Policies, legislation and regulations

BEST PRACTICE: FDI Attraction – Invest in BOGOTÁ

Bogotá is the capital and largest city of Colombia. At 2,625 meters above sea level, Bogotá is located in the center of Colombia, in the Eastern Cordillera of the Andes. With a population of almost 8 million people, the city is the political, economic, administrative, industrial, artistic and cultural center of the country. Moreover, Bogotá has the largest number of universities and research centers in the country.

Bogotá, Colombia

Source: Pixabay, CC0.

Economically, Bogotá is the main market of Colombia and the center of the most competitive region of the country. In 2017, the Bogota metropolitan region's GDP accounted for 32.4% of Colombia's total, totaling US$101.7 billion. In the same year, Bogota's per capita GDP rose to US$10,270 (Invest In Bogota, 2018). Despite important strides in reducing poverty and inequality in recent decades, these are still quite high. In 2017, the level of poverty in Bogotá was 12.4%, while the GINI Index, the most widely-used indicator to measure income inequality, remained 0.498 (DANE, 2017).

Context

- In the mid-1960s, Colombia became submerged in a major internal armed conflict, known as the Colombian conflict, between the Colombian governments, paramilitary groups, crime syndicates and far-left guerrillas. This resulted in a highly damaged international image of the country, known worldwide for its drug cartels, crime, violence and insecurity. This image had played a major role in the markets' confidence in the country.

- As part of a liberalization process in the 1990s, and in order to open the nation's economy to the global economy, Colombia adopted a series of regulatory changes that reduced international trade restrictions. This had a positive effect on the level of incoming foreign flows, both at the national level and at the local level.
- At the city level, Bogotá is strategically located in the center of the Americas, with connections to North and South America, as well as Europe. This has given the Colombian capital a strategic position as a logistical hub.

Actions

- In 2006, the investment promotion agency Invest in Bogota was envisioned. It aimed to promote the city region's positive assets as the ideal destination for foreign companies (i.e. access to South American markets, a business-friendly environment, among others).

Invest in Bogotá Slogan

- Invest in Bogota was established as a public-private partnership (PPP) between the Bogota Chamber of Commerce and the Bogota City Government, with the support of the World Bank for implementation.
- The aim of Invest in Bogota is to offer support to investors in different sectors during each stage of their investment process. Its main areas of work are: "promotion and facilitation of foreign investment," "city marketing strategy" and "improvement of the investment climate" (Invest in Bogota, 2016). Technical staff with expertise in international business, economic development, and research and analysis provide tailored support in the different sectors.
- In 2012, Invest in Bogota had an annual budget of approximately US$3 million - the City and its Chamber of Commerce each contribute 50% (Moskow, Osborn, and Leff, 2012).
- As part of the international promotion strategy of the city, a City Marketing Strategy was created to improve the image of the city as a "business-friendly city", moving away from violence and insecurity.
- Lastly, the development of free-trade zone regimes (FTZs) in Colombia has been an important instrument to attract foreign and domestic investment, by offering important fiscal incentives. One of the most successful ones is the

Zona Franca de Bogotá (ZFB), or Bogota Free Trade Zone, which offers incentives in income tax rates, VAT, duties, among others.

Outcomes

- Today, Bogotá is a leading destination for new projects of foreign direct investment coming into Latin America and Colombia. This has been the result of an active promotion strategy to attract investment, a city image campaign to restore the negative representation of the city and the establishment of fiscal incentives.

- Bogotá has taken advantage of the positive momentum of the Colombian economy and the growth of the middle class to improve the city's investment attraction strategy.

- The creation of Invest in Bogotá has been key in this process. The IPA has been very successful in attracting foreign investment to the city-region. According to the agency, **after 10 years of its establishment, from 2006 to 2016, it consolidated the development of 200 foreign projects with an estimated investment of over US$1.6 billion that generated some 21,000 direct jobs** (Invest in Bogota, 2016). On the last decade, FDI has grown on average some 30% per year.

- A study by the World Bank using FDI project data from 2003-2011 suggested that Invest in Bogota had a significant impact on the number of FDI projects that flowed into the city after the agency was created – "even after controlling for other key determinants of attracting FDI such as market size and potential, infrastructure, labor quality and security" (Hornberger, 2011). This would mean that Invest in Bogota made a difference in the flows of FDI coming to the city and the increase in private sector activity in general.

- In recent years, Invest in Bogota has received multiple awards and international recognition. For instance, it was named "best non-OECD investment promotion agency in the world" by the World Bank in 2009. Additionally, Site Selected recognized Bogotá's agency as the "Best Investment Attraction Agency from Latin America & Caribbean Regional" in 2016 and 2015. Lastly, fDi Intelligence, a service of the Financial Times that collects data on greenfield FDI, has recognized the success and work of Bogota in attracting FDI multiple occasions, including naming Bogota the "8th city with the best FDI strategy" in fDi Magazine Global Cities of the future (2015), and the "6th major American city of the future 2017/18 for FDI Strategy" in fDi American Cities of the Future 2017/18 Report.

- The Bogota Free Trade Zone, in its 20 years of operations, has attracted FDI of about US$200m and created some 90,000 direct and indirect jobs (Dettoni, 2018). More than half of its companies operate in the logistics sector, taking advantage of the strategic position of the Colombian capital with strong ties to North and South America. A growing proportion are export business services, as well as other types of businesses.
- FDI inflows to the city has had a positive impact on employment. According to estimates by Invest in Bogotá's Research and Market Intelligence area, Bogotá was the Latin American capital that generated the most employment derived from greenfield foreign investment in 2017, with a share of 2.2%, followed by Mexico City and Sao Paulo (Invest In Bogotá, 2018).

***

3.3. Attracting and Managing People Flows

Cities are centers of people flows: from visitors, to migrants, to people moving to work or study. International and diverse populations can be an important source of creativity and innovation, and incoming populations can help fill employment gaps too. So attracting investors, entrepreneurs, researchers and visitors has always been a key factor in the formulation of cities' international strategy. However, managing people's mobility is one of the biggest challenges for cities today and in the future.

3.3.1 Tourism

As discussed in Section 2, tourism is one of the world's largest industries — responsible for approximately one in 10 jobs globally and contributing over 10% to the global economy. As a result, countries and cities around the world are marketing themselves abroad in order to attract visitors. In fact, tourism has been a key priority in the urban policy agendas of many cities for quite some time. However, **mass tourism brings important challenges and can diminish the quality of life in urban areas** (See Box 2.) While attracting tourists can be a strategic tool for prosperity and development, **municipal policies must shift from seeking to attract tourists to managing them for the benefit of both local residents and visitors.**

According to the UNWTO, **sustainable tourism** can be defined as "tourism that takes full account of its current and future economic, social and environmental impacts, addressing the needs of visitors, the industry, the environment and host communities" (UNWTO, n.d.). Cities must analyze and understand their own realities and challenges regarding tourism and then implement a series of initiatives or strategies accordingly in order to achieve sustainable tourism. For instance, municipalities suffering from overtourism in city centers could promote the diversification of tourism locations across the city or region. Cities experiencing seasonal tourism in one period of the year could promote out-of-season events. Alternatively, cities experiencing high levels of low-value tourism should focus on different audiences or promote high-value activities. Overall, **local administrations should put an emphasis on making sure that urban economic development coming from tourism is redistributed and reinvested in a way that can result in an improvement in the quality of life of local communities**.

- Policies, legislation and regulations
- Change in people's behavior and preferences

BEST PRACTICE: MELBOURNE
— Becoming a Global Music City and a Cultural Destination

Melbourne is the second largest city in Australia after Sydney, which had a population of some 4.8 million people in the metropolitan area in 2017. The capital and most populous city within the state of Victoria, Melbourne encompasses the city center and a number of inner suburbs, each with its own distinctive character. With a GDP of A$324,925 million in 2017, Melbourne is the business,

Melbourne, Australia

Source: Pixabay, CC0.

administrative, cultural and recreational center of the state. The city has successfully transitioned from an economy that relied heavily on a weakening manufacturing sector to a more diversified economy with significant growth in the professional and financial and insurance services (SGS Economics and Planning, 2017).

Immigration has shaped the city since the 19th century. Melbourne's population is very diverse and multicultural, with 56% of its residents being foreign-born and around 140 cultures present in the city (City of Melbourne, 2018a). The city also has one of the highest per capita concentration of international students in the world (City of Melbourne, 2008). Melbourne has a high-quality public transportation system and nearly 480 hectares of parks and gardens.

Context

- Since the 1990s, the State of Victoria has strongly promoted the tourism industry in the region. In 1993, Tourism Victoria launched the "You'll Love Every Piece of Victoria" jigsaw campaign, which has been the longest running destination marketing campaign in the world. Melbourne, as the capital of the State of Victoria, has been a key part of many initiatives to promote tourism in the region.

- Melbourne is known nationally and internationally for its great cultural scene. Sometimes referred to as the "cultural capital" of Australia, the city is home to many cultural institutions – such as art galleries, events, festivals, street art, music and museums. It has a large number of artistic and creative industries and often hosts international events. Moreover, the city has been a global leader in the music industry for many years.

- The City of Melbourne has been investing resources in building the city's reputational brand. For instance, in 2008 the City defined a Global Positioning Statement as part of the Melbourne's Business and International Strategy 2008-2012 to enhance the city's international reputation (City of Melbourne, 2008).

Actions

- At the beginning of the 2010s, city leaders realized that the music industry and cultural industries could be important economic drivers for the city. In a 2012 census, it was found that "live music alone generated more than A$1bn in spending at small venues, concerts and festivals, supported 116,000 annual full-time equivalent jobs, and produced significant spin-off benefits to restaurants, hotels, transportation companies and other providers" in Melbourne (Terrill, Hogart, Clement, and Francis, n.d.). Moreover, there were around 120 clubs, bars and hotels with live music in Melbourne's CBD, as well as 17 larger theatres and concert venues, with around 97,000 people attending music performances in the city on Friday and Saturday nights, generating an average turnover of around $5.4 million per weekend (City of Melbourne, 2014).

- Because of the potential opportunities offered by the music industry and to support it, in 2010 the City of Melbourne developed an early Music Strategy 2010-2013 to better understand the local music industry dynamics. In 2014, the city government established a more clearly defined and ambitious strategy: "City of Melbourne Music Strategy 2014-2017." As part of the strategy, a Music Advisory Committee was approved in 2013 to provide expert advice and guidance regarding the music sector (City of Melbourne, 2014). The role of the Committee has been very important. Six goals/themes were defined: 1) visibility; 2) promotion and positioning (nationally and internationally); 3) spaces and collaboration; 4) funding and support; 5) policy reform and advocacy; and 6) research and information.

- The Music Strategy has been linked to other strategies and policies of the city, such as: "Creative City," focused on innovation and creativity; the "Prosperous City," focused on providing infrastructure and services, a highly skilled workforce and affordable business accommodation (City of Melbourne, 2014).

- At the state level, the State of Victoria has also been promoting and strengthening the music and tourism industries. For instance, in 2014, the Victorian state government introduced the "agent of change" principle, establishing regulations of the levels of noise from live music performances across Victoria, to protect live music venues in the case of new residential developers, and to reduce the potential number of complaints (Music Victoria, n.d.).

- Additionally, the state of Victoria has continued to develop regional tourism strategies and initiatives. In 2013, the "Victoria's Regional Tourism Strategy 2013-2016" was released, aiming to transform Victoria into a leading tourism and events destination in the Asia/Pacific region; to contribute to the Victorian economy; and to develop the tourism industry in the region (State of Victoria, 2013). In 2016, a new strategy was developed, the "Victorian Visitor Economy

Strategy," lays out the government's commitment to ensuring the state's growth and prosperity through tourism and events until 2025 (State of Victoria, 2017). They have defined the strategy through a process of consultation with different stakeholders.

Outcomes

- All these strategies and initiatives have had a positive effect on the tourism industry, and the music and cultural industries of Melbourne and Victoria.
- Total tourism GRP (Gross Regional Product) in the Melbourne region has increased at an average annual rate of 5.6% over the period 2006-07 to 2013-14, while total tourism employment increased at an average rate of 3.8% over the same period (Tourism Victoria, 2015). In 2015-16, the tourism sector was estimated to be worth $15.3 billion to the Melbourne region's economy (in GRP), with an increase of 10% from 2014-2015), and generated employment of approximately 126,800 people (6.0% of the region's employment) (Victoria State Government, 2017).
- The creative industries and cultural tourism contributed approximately $23 billion to the State of Victoria's economy in 2015 (BCG, 2017). Its GVA share is growing relative to the rest of the Victorian economy.
- Regarding the number of tourists received, in 2017, the city has already become a major touristic destination, receiving almost 2.8 million international visitors (Tourism Research Australia, 2018).
- The numbers of the music industry today in Melbourne are huge: the city's music industry in 2017 generated A$1.42 billion in the city; with 62,000 annual performances attracting more than 12 million patrons; having 465 live music venues; and hosting 350 music festivals (Visit Victoria, 2018). Moreover, Melbourne will be the first city in the southern hemisphere to host The Music Cities Convention.
- The Melbourne's Music Strategy 2013-2017 achieved a number of successes: celebrating Melbourne Music Week, an annual celebration held over nine days; supported local talent, by funding dozens of music-related projects; and organized the 2015 Melbourne Music Symposium, which attracted over 100 industry representatives from around the world to discuss "what makes a successful music city." Following on its success, the city has recently released the *Melbourne Music Plan 2018-21*, in order to consolidate the city's reputation as a "global music capital" (City of Melbourne, 2018b).
- These numbers consolidate Melbourne as Australia's "cultural capital" and Australia's "live music capital." The city and its metropolitan area have been

Chapter 3: Best Practices and Case Studies of Global Cities

successful in creating a positive global image and a high reputation, both nationally and internationally. The city has managed to establish its brand as "the leading sophisticated, stylish, trendy, cultural and creative city in Australia" (Victoria State Government, 2017).

Melbourne, Australia

Source: Pixabay, CC0.

- As a result of its global reputation, and its rich urban offer in arts, music, theater and gastronomy, a recent report by the Boston Consulting Group ranked Melbourne as the top cultural destination in the country, third in the Asia Pacific and 12th in the world for arts and culture (BCG, 2017).

- The city has also had highly positive results in other global city rankings. For instance, Melbourne has been considered the world's most livable city by The Economist for seven years in a row (2010-2017), although it has lost the top position to Vienna in 2018 (The Economist Intelligence Unit, 2018). The Reputation Institute's 2018 City RepTrak, ranked Melbourne number #12 in the world, although several spots down from the 2017 edition, where Melbourne was ranked #7 (Reputation Institute, 2017, 2018).

- According to estimates by BCG, cultural tourism could represent some 40% of all tourism by 2025 (up to 32% in 2017) (BCG, 2017). Moreover, estimates suggest that cultural visitors stay 25% longer than average visitors in Australia and spend 20% more per trip than visitors on average. Therefore, Melbourne's Music Strategy and Creative Strategy are aligned with Visit Victoria's objective to build Melbourne and Victoria into Australia's number one tourism destination.

- The role of the state of Victoria helping spread the music economy across different locations has also been very relevant.

- Melbourne offers a positive example of tapping into the music industry and the cultural and creative industries to improve and upgrade tourism in a city and its metropolitan area. Multi-level government support for these strategies, as well as collaboration with different stakeholders (businesses in the sector, associations, citizens, etc.), has been critical for the success of the initiatives.

New technologies and innovations, along with changes in society and in people's preferences and behavior, are giving rise to new business models and new products in the tourism industry. The co-creation of travel experiences has significantly evolved, making it easier to travel and interact with city dwellers. Cities and businesses need to promote changes in the industry that benefit both visitors and locals. New intermediators and providers have also evolved in order to match changes in consumer behavior. (See Box 7.) People are now demanding new tourism experiences and products, which creates opportunities for cities and businesses.

New business models

Change in people's behavior and preferences

BOX 7. AUTHENTICITIES, Responsible Urban Tourism

As travelers' preferences and priorities evolve, and they look for more "authentic" and "unique" experiences, tour providers and other companies in the tourism industry need to adapt and evolve to changes in society. Moreover, some travelers are increasingly demanding responsible touristic experiences that benefit both visitors and local citizens.

In this context, new companies are emerging, offering new experiences and ways of doing business in the tourism sector. Authenticitys is one of these. An online platform that connects visitors with locals, this firm offers responsible and authentic experiences within the urban tourism (Authenticitys, 2018). Together with local entrepreneurs, it co-creates and designs local experiences offered on their platform and connects visitors with these.

Authenticitys has also committed to contributing towards responsible tourism, by categorizing their impacts in six categories: Health, Education, Environment and Resources, Employability, Freedom and Equality, and Happiness (Authenticitys, 2018). The final aim is to create a positive change in the city.

This is a good example of how tourism is moving toward more responsible management and how societal changes, aided by new technologies, are helping to advance towards achieving more sustainable urban tourism with positive impact on local communities.

3.3.2 International Talent

With globalization and digitalization, talent attraction has become a key objective for economies at all levels — national, regional and local. **Cities, as hubs of economic activity, innovation and communications, have become a central player in a global competition to attract, develop and retain human capital**. Despite the rise of globalization, the "local" dimension has become increasingly important for talent attraction. Cities tend to be more open to people, ideas and knowledge, than rural areas, which further attracts international talent, students, scholars and innovators. This, at the same time, is associated with more innovative and competitive sectors.

However, some cities lack the number of high-skilled workers required in today's knowledge and service economy. Thus, if cities want to remain competitive in the current international context, local governments need to design and implement policies and plans to attract, develop and retain international talent.

Many elements attract skilled workers, including having a favorable labor and business environment, high quality of life and a wide range of cultural and leisure offerings. While there is no single recipe for success, city managers can design favorable conditions to draw talented people. For instance, designing attractive tax and regulatory environments; cultivating the city's talent ecosystem; stimulating the growth of new businesses and start-ups; or providing a welcome information service and landing support for new residents.

Policies, legislation and regulations

BOX 8. Incentives for attracting skilled workers: The case of Zurich

The city of Zurich, despite having a relatively small population with over 400,000 inhabitants in the city proper and around 1.5 million people in the metropolitan area (Müller, 2019), has managed to become one of the most important business and financial centers in the world. The finance sector contributes to around one-third of the city's wealth, as well as a quarter of its employment (Stadt Zürich, 2019b). In addition to being a global leader in the banking and finance sectors, the canton of Zurich has also a great diversity of well-developed service-based sectors and industries, including business services, research and development, life sciences, the creative economy and the tourism sector.

All of these key sectors are knowledge-based sectors that require skilled labor. High skilled economic sectors tend to be highly productive and competitive sectors. In fact, according to a report by INSEAD (2019), Switzerland led the 2019 Global Talent Competitiveness Index, while Zurich ranked 5th in the Global City Talent Competitiveness Index. The country performs particularly well in proving a favorable and business and labor landscape, a special focus on lifelong learning, and the capacity for retaining talent, thanks to good pension and social protection systems, among others. As a result, the Zurich canton is the country's economic powerhouse, contributing around one-fifth of the country's total GDP in 2016 (Bundesamt für Statistik, 2018).

Zurich, Switzerland

Source: Pixabay, C00.

The city of Zurich has been able to attract businesses and employees in these sectors internationally for a number of reasons, including its attractive employment and educational opportunities, favorable working policies, high quality of life, and entrepreneurial environment. For instance, as of April 2019, the unemployment rate in the city of Zurich stood at just 2.3% (Stadt Zürich, 2019a), reflecting the significant number of employment opportunities in the city. Additionally, employment policies – both at the national level and at the city level – favor flexibility, offer an attractive tax and regulatory climate for international talent, and have good working conditions, including fair salaries and advantageous social benefits, diverse working time models, equal opportunities for men and women, a wide variety of educational and training opportunities. (Stadt Zürich, 2019b).

The city of Zurich also provides a high quality of life and strong cultural dynamism. The consulting firm Mercer has for many years ranked the Swiss city among the top cities in its renowned Quality of Living City Ranking, in which Zurich was ranked 2nd in the 2019 ranking (Mercer, 2019). In addition, Zurich also offers a quality education system, with a large number of higher education institutions, including two universities featured in the top 100 of QS World Rankings 2019 (Top Universities, 2019), and an advantageous and innovative entrepreneurship environment, which also attracts international students, researchers and entrepreneurs.

In order to facilitate the integration of newly arrived citizens to city, the City of Zurich created the Integration Office. It coordinates issues related to integration and migration and provides information, courses and advice for new residents, which is available in more than 10 different languages, as well as organizes welcoming events (City of Zurich, 2019). There is also a Welcome Desk that offers personal advisory services for newcomers.

All of these abovementioned elements combined – such as a favorable business and employment landscape, a good quality of life, and welcome services – have increased the city's attractiveness to international workers. This is especially relevant in service-based and knowledge-based sectors, which attract a huge number of international skilled labor and are the most developed sectors in the city's economy. As a result, Zurich is a global leading business center today, with a highly diverse and multicultural population, with more than 30% of the population foreign-born (Nguyen, 2017).

3.3.3 Migration and Refugees

Cities, as the main destinations of migrants, will face the greatest challenges of global migration. First, when migrants or refugees arrive in a city, they need to access city services and urban amenities to cover basic needs. This increases the pressure on city services and infrastructures, which are often already very limited, especially in cities in developing countries. Second, the formation of segregated community groups or ethnic enclaves within a city, and the increase of racism and xenophobia, can exacerbate integration and social cohesion challenges.

However, migration also results in diverse populations, which tends to trigger talent, innovation and creativity, boosting economic and urban development. Some of the most well-known global cities, such as London, New York, Istanbul and Hong Kong have all received large numbers of immigrants (Clark, 2016). They have also hosted refugees and asylum seekers. These diverse populations have greatly contributed to the urban development of the cities where they have settled.

Through some of the key levers of change, such as policy reforms, urban planning or changes in people's behavior, particularly community perception and engagement, local policymakers can transform the potential challenges brought by immigration into positive ones, such as filling labor gaps or developing integrated development and community engagement.

BEST PRACTICE: ATHENS
— Working together to promote migrant and refugee integration

Policies, legislation and regulations

Athens, Greece

Athens is the capital and largest city of Greece and one of the oldest cities in the world. Located in the Attica region on the Balkan Peninsula, Athens is the southernmost capital on the European mainland. The city proper has a population of some 665,000 inhabitants; while the Athens Metropolitan Area, with over 55 municipalities, is home to some 3.8 million people. The metropolitan area includes the city of Pireaus, one of the largest passenger ports in Europe.

Source: Pixabay, CC0.

Today Athens is a cosmopolitan metropolis and the cultural, economic and political center of Greece. In 2016, the GDP per capita of the Metropolitan Athens was US$36,850 (Open Data Network, 2018). Tourism is an important economic sector in Greece, supporting over 11% of the national employment (Sharecity, 2017). The 2009 financial crisis deeply affected both Greece and Athens, resulting in drastic austerity measures, decreases in GDP and rising unemployment. Youth employment in the Attica region reached 46.5% in 2016 and over 20% of the population is considered to be at risk of poverty (Sharecity, 2017).

Context

- Traditionally, Greece has been a country of emigration. However, during the 1970s and 1980s, it started receiving migration flows from Philippines and Central and Eastern Europe, with Albanians being one of the largest groups. More recently, the city has also received migration from Asia (Pakistan, India, Afghanistan) and Africa (Maghreb region and sub-Saharan Africa).

- Today, 40% of the foreign population living in Greece reside in the municipality of Athens, making up 19% of the city's population (Sharecity, 2017).
- Due to the European refugee crisis, which started in the beginning of 2015, Greece has experienced a huge increase both in the number of arrivals of refugees and in the number of refugee applications, mainly from Syria, Pakistan and Afghanistan.
- In 2015 alone, over 500,000 people transited through the port of Piraeus in Athens, often spending a few days in the city (Eurocities, 2016).
- As of March 2016, Greece had some 50,000 refugees. One-third – or more than 15,000 – stayed in Athens (WEF, 2017). This was putting a severe pressure on the city's services and infrastructures and on the city government, which was already struggling because of the ongoing financial crisis.

Actions

- Many of the refugees arriving in Athens aim to use the city as a transitional hub to access other countries in Europe. However, many of them remain temporarily or permanently in the city and there is a need to integrate them. To achieve this goal, several actions have been taken.
- First, in order to provide temporary shelters and housing, the city of Athens collaborated with international organizations and institutions, such as the UNHCR and the European Commission's ECHO (European Civil Protection and Humanitarian Aid Operations), among other partners, to offer temporary shelters and, as of 2017, had plans to build 20,000-30,000 houses in the following years (WEF, 2017). The humanitarian partners pay the rent and the city council pays the utilities and other expenses.
- Second, in terms of education and healthcare, through the collaboration of different partners, Greek, English and other language training is being offered. For instance, the municipality of Athens offers Greek language lessons (WEF, 2017). Moreover, the "open schools" program was created to open 25 schools during afterschool hours to organize activities such as language courses, cooking classes, or music lessons, aimed at both migrants and refugee parents and their children, with support from philanthropic organizations (Eurocities, 2017).
- Additionally, in October 2016 an initiative led by the mayor of Athens, Giorgos Kaminis, called Solidarity Cities, was launched by the City of Athens and in the framework of the EUROCITIES network in order to constitute a structure through which different cities collaborate to address the challenge of refugee management and integration (Solidarity Cities, 2018).

- Under the same EUROCITIES network, another project called CITIES-GroW, started in 2017 to provide practical advice to municipal leaders and decision-makers in Europe regarding the integration of migrants through economic activity in cities. The project is carried out through a mentorship/implementer scheme, in which Athens is partnering with the city of Munich (Germany) to facilitate access to the refugee labor market (Eurocities, 2018).

- In June 2017, the Athens Coordination Center for Migrant and Refugee issues (ACCMR) was created with a founding donor, the Stavros Niarchos Foundation, and coordination led by the Athens Partnership, through the Vice-Mayor's Office for Migrants and Refugees. The ACCMR aims to facilitate the integration of migrants and refugees through an efficient coordination between all the different stakeholders operating within the city to support initiatives in the protection and integration of migrants and refugees, such as the municipal authorities, national and international NGOs, international organizations, and migrant and refugee community groups. With this objective, the ACCMR has developed a Strategic Action Plan for the integration of migrants and refugees in the city, and works with other cities to exchange and transfer know-how (City of Athens, n.d.).

- Within this framework, the Athens Observatory on Migrant and Refugee issues (AORI) was established as a pilot research program (2016-2017) to better understand the demographic and social characteristics of the refugees staying in Athens, and the public opinion and perceptions of the city's residents towards refugees. This will allow developing more accurate policies and initiatives accordingly. Lastly, a digital platform was created to offer information and facilitate cooperation.

Athens, Greece

Source: Pixabay, CC0.

Outcomes

- As of 2017, some 6,000 houses of the planned housing system were already used by refugees (WEF, 2017).
- As of summer 2016, 1,250 participants, of whom 450 were refugees, took part in the "open schools" program activities (Eurocities, 2017).
- Collaboration and cooperation among the different stakeholders involved, as well as with other municipalities and international actors, has been essential for the design and implementation of cohesion and integration policies.
- The city is still struggling to manage the huge number of migrants and refugees arriving to the city, but it is now taking a more proactive approach to understand the different communities living in Athens today in order to implement more effective solutions and initiatives.
- The creation of a specific municipal body dedicated to migrant/refugees has also been very important.

***

3.4. City's Soft Power Attributes

Soft power refers to the ability to obtain preferred outcomes by attraction rather than coercion or payment (Nye, 2017). Joseph Nye first coined the term "soft power" in the 1990s to describe the ability of a country to attract and persuade others to do what it wants without the use of force or coercion. This latter form of aggressive or coercive political power, such as the use of a country's economic and military power, is defined as "hard power." The term "soft power" is now widely used in international relations and foreign policy, not only for countries but also for cities or regional governments.

A city's soft power attributes include all those aspects that make a city attractive: culture, music, arts and literature, architecture, food, sports, tourism, cultural diversity, education, research, and many others features or characteristics that make the city's identity unique and attractive to a diversity of people and business and entrepreneurs alike. Understanding the value of a city's soft power attributes is critical for achieving all of the above-mentioned city international objectives: to attract and retain people and organizations; improve a city's image and reputation; and increase its influence in the global arena. These all have the final aim of increasing city dwellers' wellbeing and fostering prosperity.

3.4.1. Culture, Arts and Entertainment

Culture is a major engine for urbanization, economic development and a major magnet for people flows, either in the form of tourism or short and long-term migration. **Culture in its different fields as art, architecture, design, music, sports, films or cuisine, is not only an important instrument for growth in cities but also a central attribute of a metropolis' soft power**. As a way of example, in the field of music, the song and music video "Gangnam Style" was viewed and heard all over the world. This song put the Gangnam neighborhood and the city of Seoul in the map for many people who consequently wanted to visit this location. In the area of sports, the FC Barcelona and Real Madrid football teams make important contributions to these Spanish cities' international reputation and image.

From urban heritage to museums, galleries and art facilities, music halls, theaters, architecture or restaurants and cafés, **improving the cultural amenities of a city increases its attractiveness for tourists, expatriates and locals alike**. City managers need to design and promote a city's cultural industry that is attractive both for its inhabitants and for the different city users and visitors (tourists, migrants, creatives, international students, etc.). For instance, the city of Bilbao in Spain is a good example of a city using a strategy of architectural production. In particular, the Guggenheim Museum of Bilbao, is a key element of the city's revitalization plan to raise Bilbao's international profile to attract businesses and tourism.

```
Infrastructure and        Change in people's        New business
urban planning            behavior and              models
                          preferences
```

BEST PRACTICE: BUSAN'S Gamcheon Culture Village
– From a refugee shelter to an international tourist attraction.

Saha-gu, Busan, South Korea

Source: Pixabay, CC0.

Located on the southeastern tip of the Korean peninsula, Busan is South Korea's second largest city after Seoul, with a population of approximately 3.5 million residents. The city is an economic, cultural and educational center, with a GDP in the metropolitan area of US$133,617.8 million (PPP, 2017) (Euromonitor International, 2017a). Economically, the city is one of the most important maritime logistics hubs in Northeast Asia. The Port of Busan is the largest container-handling port in the country and the fifth busiest port in the world, processing 19.85 million TEU of container cargo volume in 2016 (World Shipping Council, n.d.). Additionally, the MICE (Meetings, Incentives, Conferences, and Exhibitions) and tourism industries are also very important.

Context

- Gamcheon Village started as a shantytown or slum built by Korean War Refugees in the 1950s on the slope of Mt. Cheonmasan, with steep streets and narrow twisting alleys. Houses were small and residents had to share public restrooms.

- In the 1960s, Gamcheon had some 30,000 residents in about 1,000 terraced shanties (Hong and Lee, 2015). However, by the end of last century, and despite Korea's and Busan's fast-growing economies, Gamcheon Village had fallen behind. The area was one of the poorest and most underdeveloped parts of Busan, with its deficiency score being the second highest out of a total

of 205 villages examined in Busan (Guangzhou International Award for Urban Innovation., 2018).
- By 2010, its population had decrease to about 8,000 people (while the rate of senior citizens increased to 26%), and the remaining population was composed mainly of the poorest and most vulnerable citizens (Guangzhou International Award for Urban Innovation., 2018). Therefore, Gamcheon village was one of the most underdeveloped parts of Busan and at risk of disappearing.

Actions

- Within this context, the *Gamcheon Culture Village* project was born. The Saha Municipal District, or *Saha-gu,* where Gamcheon is located, aimed at alleviating the degeneration of the area by implementing an urban regeneration program, making use of the unique characteristics of the village, such as its distinctive landscape and some artistic movements already happening in the area. The objective was to give a boost to the area, enhance the local economy and promote tourism.
- The renewal process started in 2009, when the Korea's Ministry of Culture, Sports, and Tourism called on artists in the *Village Art Project Competition* to decorate the village with murals, sculptures and other artworks. The residents of the Gamcheon Village won the competition, obtaining 100 million won (about US$95,000) of funding for the project called *"Dreaming of Machu Picchu in Busan"*[15] (Hong and Lee, 2015).

Artwork in Gamcheon Culture Village

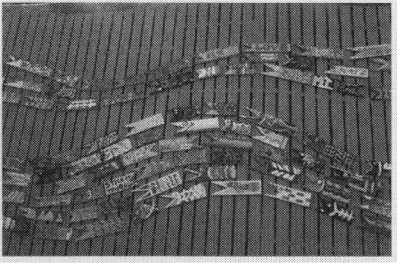

Source: Ana Duch.

- After this first project, the regeneration process of the *Gamcheon Culture Village* continued through different initiatives. For instance, the "Maze–Maze Project" was implemented to fill empty houses with art works and to connect

---

[15] Gamcheon is usually referred to as the "Machu Picchu of Korea" because of its steep hills.

the alleys (Hong and Lee, 2015). Several arts and cultural projects have been developed, including the installation of 66 pieces of artwork throughout the neighborhood; the opening of 17 art galleries; the inauguration of an outdoor event venue for cultural performances, exhibitions, and festivals; or the creation of various educational programs to enhance the residents' cultural capacity (Culture 21, UCLG, and Ciudad de México, 2009).

- As part of the redevelopment of the area, most of the budget was devoted to extensive construction and infrastructure works, such as improvement of the sewage system, natural gas pipelines and communal septic tanks (Guangzhou International Award for Urban Innovation., 2018).

- The project received funding both from the Busan city government and from the Korean government. A creative city task force team was created, including 17 local officials and some 40 local artists, village activity planners and professors (Ibid).

- Moreover, active participation of the different stakeholders, including residents, public institutions, the private sector and professional artists has been key for the success of the project through a process of co-creation. A resident council was organized to encourage participation. It included a village business project group for private profitable economic activities such as coffees and restaurants; a service group to conduct guided tours; and a public relations group for promotion of the project (Hong and Lee, 2015).

Outcomes

- From 2009 to 2017, the project received a total budget of US$9,400,000 (Guangzhou International Award for Urban Innovation., 2018).

- The village has turned itself into a major tourist destination, by hosting a variety of cultural events and art exhibitions, and receiving approximately 2 million visitors annually (Culture 21 et al., 2009).

- The brand identity of Gamcheon has been developed nationally and internationally.

- Most importantly, the Gamcheon community has enhanced its living conditions after the project. Around 8,000 residents saw their living conditions improve, while some 200 people found jobs as new souvenir shops, restaurants and cafés opened, and new touristic activities appeared (Guangzhou International Award for Urban Innovation., 2018).

- The project can be understood as a business model for job creation and local economic redevelopment.
- The governance system of the project, through residents' participation and co-creation processes, such as participation-based public art projects or communal commercial businesses, has been key for its success.
- The *Gamcheon Culture Village* project has gained international recognition as a benchmark for urban regeneration initiatives, and has received multiple awards, such as the first Excellent City Award at International Association of Educating Cities (IAEC), the UNESCO Education for Sustainable Development Certification of Official Project, and the 2016 ROK President's Award at Korea Space Award Grand Prize at Asian Townscape Awards.

Gamcheon Culture Village

Source: Ana Duch.

3.4.2 International Events

Hosting high-profile international events – including sport mega-events, such as the Olympic Games or the FIFA World Cup; international political events such as UN international conferences or G-summits; or international exhibitions as the World Expos – **can provide opportunities for gaining international visibility and reputation and improve the city's built environment and operations**.

First of all, big international events with significant media presence can help boost a city's global image and serve as an advertisement platform for the city to the world. These global events have the potential to improve the city's prestige and reputation by demonstrating that the city is able to host logistically complex events and do it successfully. Second, mega-events also promote unquestionable transformations in the cities where they take place. Big events often entail an upgrade in the city's built environment, with the construction of new infrastructures and facilities. They also require a high level of logistic and strategic complexity that have the potential to improve the dynamics and operations of the city. For a big international event to work successfully, efficient execution of the different urban systems and their services is often required, and this often involves an improvement of the skills of local governments, business and populations. However, big events – in particular major sport events that require big financial commitments and great investments – can also bring great risks. (See Box 9.)

BOX 9. How Big Sport Events Can Boost a City's International Outreach

International sporting events can significantly increase a city's international outreach and prompt urban development. Sport mega-events, such as the Olympic Games, the FIFA World Cup, the Open of tennis, or Formula One, can be a good opportunity to project a city's positive image in the international arena, increase its global visibility and improve its reputation. For instance, the Formula One Grands Prix for Bahrain or the Australian Open Grand Slam of tennis for Melbourne have served as marketing campaigns at the international level to increase visibility and attract visitors.

Additionally, these types of events can also help increase and restore the city's global reputation. For instance, the Olympic Games of Tokyo in 1964, Mexico City in 1968, or Seoul in 1988, are examples of cities aiming to project a global image of "advanced" and modern cities at that time by demonstrating that they were able to successfully host such complex mega events (Rivenburgh, 2010).

As previously mentioned, "big sports events" not only serve as city marketing and reputation campaigns, but they can also result in big improvements in economic development and urban transformation. For instance, a well-known example is Barcelona, Spain. In 1992, the Olympic games triggered urban redevelopment and local growth, providing best practices for developing new infrastructure, improving the local economy and marking Barcelona as a leading tourism destination.

The Olympic Games are thus the ultimate mega sporting event at the city level, due to the millions of spectators and large media presence involved. Most of today's global cities have hosted the Olympic Games in previous years, and some of them haven even hosted them on multiple occasions, such as London, Paris, Los Angeles or soon Tokyo. Hosting the Olympic Games often carries a lot of prestige and international visibility. It is a great window display to the world to promote, position and brand the city as a global destination. Moreover, it also has the potential to offer important economic benefits. Sports mega events such as the Olympic Games offer important positive externalities to the city and its citizens, due to the building of new facilities, the improvement of existing infrastructures, and the generation of new local business opportunities and the increase of employment levels.

Tokyo 2020

However, big sports events also entail high levels of investments and construction costs, and may result in public sector indebtedness, high maintenance liabilities, increases in property rentals, rises in employment and business activities that are also temporary, among many other negative consequences. For instance, nearly half of the Olympic Games since 1960 have ended up costing more than twice as much as expected (Aleem, 2018). Therefore, cities hosting this kind of large sporting event should take advantage of the opportunity to increase the city's international outreach to a global audience, and other opportunities resulting from it. They should also try to target investment and spend not only what is needed for the big event but also for the local economy.

***

3.5. Cities as International Actors

Globalization brings along critical global challenges. However, most of the impacts and effects of those global challenges are local. As cities grow in terms of population, wealth and power, they want **to play a more relevant**

role, responding to current global challenges and to gain voice, influence and recognition in international forums and global debates. City leaders want to be able to impact local, regional and global policy in order to drive the city's agenda and to meet the needs and challenges of their citizens.

City Diplomacy and City Networks

Diplomacy and foreign affairs have traditionally been tools for national governments. However, cities are increasingly acting as global actors in their own right. City diplomacy can be defined as "the institutions and processes by which cities engage in relations with actors on an international political stage, with the aim of representing themselves and their interests to one another" (van der Pluijm, 2007). This can be done through different processes or structures. For instance, there is a growing professionalization of cities' international activities, with cities around the world creating specific positions and offices for foreign policy and international relations, such as the Mayor's Office of International Affairs of Los Angeles or New York City. The main aim of this type of office is to expand the city's connections at an international level in order to promote trade and foreign investment, or to cooperate on issues such as the sharing of ideas and initiatives to fight climate change or on how to implement the SDGs.

Another way for cities to increase their international outreach is **to engage more directly in international organizations and supranational bodies to gain voice and influence in them**. For instance, the European Committee of the Regions (CoR) is an EU advisory body composed of local and regional governments to give voice to regions and cities in the European Union. Another example is the Urban 20 (U20) initiative, developed in 2017, under the leadership of the mayor of the City of Buenos Aires and the mayor of Paris, with the aim of raising the profile of urban issues within the G20 agenda. The aim of these organizations is to be included in major decisions in international politics.

However, perhaps the most relevant way in which cities cooperate internationally is when they gather together in **city networks or city platforms** to tackle specific global challenges. As previously mentioned in Section 2.4, cities are increasingly engaging in diverse forms of city-to-city collaboration, such as sister cities and city networks. New technologies and digitalization have eased connections across borders, allowing local governments from different parts of the world to increasingly work together through these international city platforms or networks. Tables 7A and 7B in Section 2 show a number of international city networks in different fields that address global issues affecting cities locally. An important example of the power of cities working collectively to tackle global challenges is in the area of global environmental governance and fighting climate change, as exhibited in Box 10.

Policies, legislation and regulations

BOX 10. Cities taking the lead in climate change governance

Environmental challenges such as climate change and pollution are global in nature, but their origins and impacts are local. As mentioned in our previous book volume, *Cities and the Environment*, cities are responsible for some 60% to 80% of global energy consumption and generate around 70% of the world's greenhouse gas (GHG) emissions (Berrone, Ricart, and Duch T-Figueras, 2016). Moreover, they consume around 75% of natural resources and generate around 50-60% of global waste. As the number of people living in cities increases, urban areas will continue to put more and more stress on the environment. In fact, cities are often considered key "guilty parties" of environmental degradation, since traditional urban lifestyles contribute to increased traffic leading to CO_2 emissions, high resource consumption and high levels of waste generation, among other effects.

However, cities can also be part of the solution. Urban areas have the potential to offer more innovative and sustainable production and consumption models that take advantage of economies of scale and proximity spillovers that take place in cities. As a result, there is increasing awareness of the importance of local action in tackling global environmental challenges. A concentration of skills, knowledge and resources can be found in cities, so they can be centers for driving sustainability. In this sense, cities should take coordinated action beyond national frameworks, and share and exchange knowledge, skills and best practices.

In fact, cities around the world are increasingly coming together to pool resources, set agendas and share experiences related to global climate change. In a study by Keiner and Kim (2007) it was found that from 1982 to 2004, the number of sustainability-related city networks rose from eight to 49. In a more recent 2015 study that analyzed 170 city networks, it was found that 29% of the total networks were focused on the topic of the environment, followed by poverty, gender and inequality (22.8%), energy (12.4%) and peacebuilding (10.6%) (Acuto and Rayner, 2016). These studies indicate that cities are increasingly working together to achieve greater sustainability outcomes and fight against climate change and its negative consequences.

Many of the largest city networks by membership are in the areas of combating climate change and protecting the environment (see Table 7A). For instance, a well-known example is the international network C40, a worldwide city network of 94 mega-cities representing more than 700 million people with the goal of combatting climate change. C40 was originally launched in 2006 with 40 cities as a city diplomacy strategy for sharing knowledge and developing city-to-city cooperation to empower cities to undertake climate action initiatives, in particular reducing GHG (Chan, 2016). In 15 years, the network has more than doubled its membership, collectively taken thousands of local climate actions and gained international recognition. Moreover, it is the driving force behind The Compact of Mayors, which in 2016 joined forces with the Covenant of Mayors to create the Global Covenant of Mayors for Climate and Energy, which focuses on climate mitigation and adaptation (C40, 2019).

The main aim of these kinds of urban networks is to bring cities together voluntarily, foster collaboration, share experiences, exchange ideas and support leadership. Transnational city networks focusing on sustainability have become a useful tool for local governments seeking to learn how to design and implement a wide range of successful policy interventions, such as implementing low carbon mobility initiatives, building retrofitting programs or energy efficient public lighting, reducing emissions and preserving the environment. For instance, as of 2015, 30% of all climate actions in the city network C40 were being delivered through city-to-city collaboration (c40 and Arup, 2015). This exhibits how cooperation and coordination works at the city level. Moreover, city networks also serve as a monitoring instrument to keep track of progress, since many cities report their emissions reductions to other cities as a task of their city-network commitments (Gordon and Johnson, 2018).

The proliferation of city networks focused on sustainability and climate action over the past two decades suggests that local administrations are becoming more important in terms of environmental global governance. As previously mentioned, cities are the main contributors to climate change, but they are also highly vulnerable. Thus, cities want to be active players in overcoming the current global environmental challenges.

City networks have thus become influential players in global governance issues having a considerable impact on policy design and implementation. For instance, when the Trump administration announced their intention to withdraw the United States from the Paris Agreement in 2017, many U.S. cities and states raised their voices. Through platforms such as the U.S. Climate Alliance and the Climate Mayors, they announced they would commit to the emission reductions stipulated by the Paris Agreement.

City networks are therefore very important elements for city diplomacy. However, the rapidly growing and vast number of city networks emerging in recent decades also complicates the growth of governance structures. As a result, cities need to engage in city networks strategically, to take advantage of the benefits they offer, while reducing weaknesses associated with them, mainly due to potential overlaps (Acuto, Morissette and Tsouros, 2017).

Cities and Political Power

Lastly, **another way to increase a city's international outreach and its global connections is by becoming centers of international politics or homes to international bodies and international organizations**. In fact, the establishment of international organization offices in cities can boost their international reputation and visibility, while helping them stimulate economic growth and urban development (See Box 11).

BOX 11. Cities as Hubs of International Politics and International Organizations

Cities are not only the centers of national politics, but they also host embassies, consulates and international organizations, giving them more exposure and connections with the global stage. The following are examples of important urban powerhouses hosting institutions with international outreach.

Washington D.C., USA

Washington D.C. is not only the capital of the United States and a hub of political activity, but it is also the largest urban concentration of international organizations and think tanks in the world, including the headquarters of both the International Monetary Fund (IMF) and the World Bank, as well as the well-known Brookings Institution (Coombs, 2012).

Brussels, Belgium

Brussels is the heart of political Europe, hosting the main institutions of the European Union (EU), such as the European Commission, the European Parliament and the European Council. It is also home to important international institutions, such as the North Atlantic Treaty Organization (NATO) and the World Customs Organisation (WCO).

Brussels, Belgium

Geneva, Switzerland

Geneva, a key global political player, has had a long tradition of hosting international organizations. It hosts the headquarters of more than 25 intergovernmental organizations, international institutions or secretariats - including the International Committee of the Red Cross, the International Labour Organization, the World Health Organization and the World Trade Organization, as well as various other quasi-governmental international organizations (Confédération suisse, 2019). As a result, Geneva has become a key actor in international cooperation and multilateral diplomacy.

Nairobi, Kenya

A last example, which is outside the traditional western dominance of international organizations, is Nairobi. The city hosts many international organizations such as the United Nations Environment Programme (UNEP) and the United Nations Human Settlement Programme (UN-Habitat), among others. The presence of these organizations has helped the Kenyan capital to develop and become one of the most important urban centers in East Africa.

***

4. Concluding Remarks

Cities have traditionally opened the doors to the world. From the ancient trading cities to modern networked global cities, urban areas are usually the gateways to other markets, arrival and departure points of migrants and global centers of information, innovation and knowledge flows. Thus, the role of cities as hubs of "connections and exchanges" is not new. However, the latest technological advances and ICTs have intensified communications and connectivity at all levels, allowing for more and deeper exchanges.

With rising urbanization and technology-driven globalization, cities' international outreach is expanding as never before. Today's higher levels of urban connectedness have led to economic, political, cultural and societal changes that give **cities a new central role in the architecture of global networks of exchange**. Cities today are the nodal points of cross-border flows of people, goods, capital and knowledge, and this increased connectivity results in broader and deeper ties between cities that can bring important economic, social and cultural developments and opportunities.

However, greater globalization also increases global competition for resources and opportunities, which can result in important negative effects. In fact, as discussed in Section 2, some of the largest and more open cities of the world are also the most unequal. Therefore, **urban managers and local policymakers need to design and implement global strategies, policies and plans that will allow them to take advantage of the newly intensified centrality of cities at the international level.** These should also help them reap the benefits brought by increased connectivity and globalization, while dealing with the negative effects of increased competition. It is in cities' best interest to expand their international outreach in order to promote their local interests to the world and to position themselves more effectively within the international sphere, with the final aim of improving their local realities and the quality of life of their citizens.

Section 3 covered different initiatives and strategies that cities around the world are designing and implementing to unleash their external potential. For instance, in order to stimulate international trade and attract foreign investments – and to take advantage of the economic opportunities offered at the international level – urban managers are setting up specific trade and investment agencies for international promotion. City leaders are also defining more comprehensive global strategies, as well as investing in improving their cities' image and reputation. This is vital for increasing a city's attractiveness, stimulating trade and investment, attracting international visitors, and drawing and retaining international talent. The capacity to act in a coordinated and collaborative way is crucial for the city's international strategy to succeed.

Not only is the number of exchanges taking place in cities rising, the scope of influence and power of cities on the international stage is being transformed. As the limits between the local and the global become gradually blurred, **a new balance of power between different actors** – national governments, supra-national bodies, cities, networks and organizations, etc. – **is emerging** in different ways. First, state-power is decentralizing, giving regions and cities greater importance. Second, non-state actors, especially cities, are raising their voices, asking for more power and influence in regard to global issues. Most of the most critical global challenges of today - such as climate change, inequality or poverty - are global in nature, yet their effects are local. Therefore, **cities are** demanding to play a more relevant role in overcoming the world's most critical challenges.

Increased connectivity has allowed cities to better communicate and coordinate among themselves. This has resulted in an explosion of **global city networks** in recent decades. City networks provide platforms where cities can cooperate on different issues — such as climate change, energy or transportation — and share and exchange ideas and initiatives. They are also tools that allow cities to act more strategically at the international level and to become more relevant actors in global governance. As urban areas continue to host greater concentrations of people, economic power and resources, **the role of cities as key actors in global governance will become more prominent.**

As a result, the ability of urban policymakers and city leaders to manage the city's international outreach and adapt to changes in the global arena will be critical for ensuring the future prosperity of cities and the well-being of their inhabitants. Greater connectivity, networking, coordination and strategy-sharing will be key for cities seeking to adopt solutions to today's most pressing global challenges.

5. References

Acuto, M., Decramer, H., Kerr, J., Klaus, I., Tabory, S., and Toly, N. (2018). Toward City Diplomacy: Assessing capacity in select global cities. Chicago: The Chicago Council on Global Affairs.

Acuto, M., Morissette, M., and Tsouros, A. (2017). City Diplomacy: Towards More Strategic Networking? Learning with WHO Healthy Cities. *Global Policy*, *8*(1), 14–22.

Acuto, M., and Rayner, S. (2016). City networks: Breaking gridlocks or forging (new) lock-ins? *International Affairs*, *92*(5), 1147–1166.

Ajuntament de Barcelona (2017). *Barcelona tourism activity report*. Retrieved from https://ajuntament.barcelona.cat/turisme/sites/default/files/1_turisme_estadistiques_2017_caps1.pdf

Aleem, Z. (2018). Why (almost) no one wants to host the Olympics anymore. Retrieved February 21, 2019, from https://www.vox.com/world/2018/2/23/17008910/2018-winter-olympics-host-stadiums-cost-pyeongchang

Anttiroiko, A. V. (2015). City branding as a response to global intercity competition. *Growth and Change*, *46*(2), 233–252.

Armbrecht, A. (2016). Where are the global cities of the future? World Economic Forum (WEF). Retrieved from https://www.weforum.org/agenda/2016/02/who-has-the-largest-migrant-population/

ATKearney (2019). *A Question of Talent: How Human Capital Will Determine the Next Global Leaders - 2019 Global Cities Report*. Retrieved from https://www.atkearney.com/documents/20152/2794549/A+Question+of+Talent—2019+Global+Cities+Report.pdf/106f30b1-83db-25b3-2802-fa04343a36e4?t=1561389512018

Authenticitys (2018). About us I Authenticitys. Retrieved August 10, 2018, from https://www.authenticitys.com/en/about-us/

References

Barcelona Global (n.d.) Barcelona Global. Retrieved August 9, 2018, from https://www.barcelonaglobal.org/about-us/

BCG (2017). *Melbourne as a Global Cultural Destination Final Report (Summary)*. Melbourne. Retrieved from http://apo.org.au/system/files/95526/apo-nid95526-346156.pdf

Behrens, K., and Robert-Nicoud, F. (2014). Urbanisation makes the world more unequal - VOX, CEPR Policy Portal. Retrieved October 8, 2018, from https://voxeu.org/article/inequality-big-cities

Berkes, E., and Gaetani, R. (2018). *Income Segregation and Rise of the Knowledge Economy* (Working paper). Retrieved from https://www.tse-fr.eu/sites/default/files/TSE/documents/sem2018/Jobmarket2018/JMP/berkes_jmp.pdf

Berrone, P., Ricart, J.-E., and Duch T-Figueras, A. I. (2016). *Cities and the Environment: The challenge of becoming green and sustainable*. CreateSpace.

Berrone, P., Ricart, J.-E., and Duch T-Figueras, A. I. (2017). *Cities and the Economy: Fueling Growth, Jobs and Innovation*. CreateSpace.

Berrone, P., Ricart, J. E., Duch, A. and Carrasco, C. (2019). *IESE Cities in Motion Index 2019*. http://doi.org/10.15581/018.ST-509

Berrone, P., Ricart, J. E., and Carrasco, C. (2014). What City Has the Best Image ? An Analysis of Media Coverage of 20 Large Cities. *IESE Occasional Paper, ST-326-E*.

Berrone, P., Ricart, J. E., and Duch, A. I. (2017). *Cities & Social Cohesion: Designing More Inclusive Urban Areas*. (IESE Cities in Motion: International Urban Best Practices; Vol. 4). CreateSpace.

Berube, A. (2018). City and metropolitan income inequality data reveal ups and downs through 2016 - Brookings Institution. Retrieved October 8, 2018, from https://www.brookings.edu/research/city-and-metropolitan-income-inequality-data-reveal-ups-and-downs-through-2016/

Bristol City Council (2018). *Bristol: Global City*. Retrieved from https://www.bristol.gov.uk/documents/20182/2053023/Bristol+International+Strategy/da9a5464-4f28-5591-715c-27d401ab4992

Bundesamt für Statistik (2018). Bruttoinlandsprodukt (BIP) nach Grossregion und Kanton - 2008-2016. Retrieved July 9, 2019, from https://www.bfs.admin.ch/bfs/de/home/statistiken/volkswirtschaft/volkswirtschaftliche-gesamtrechnung/bruttoinlandprodukt-kanton.assetdetail.6369918.html

C40 (2019). Compact of Mayors. Retrieved July 11, 2019, from https://www.c40.org/programmes/compact-of-mayors

c40, and Arup (2015). *Climate Action in Megacities 3.0*. Retrieved from www.c40.org

Chan, D. K. -h. (2016). City diplomacy and "glocal" governance: Revitalizing cosmopolitan democracy. *Innovation: The European Journal of Social Science Research, 29*(2), 134–160.

Cheer, J. M., Novelli, M., and Milano, C. (2018). How "overtourism" is affecting cities. Retrieved October 18, 2018, from https://www.sbs.com.au/news/how-overtourism-is-affecting-cities

Chicago Council on Global Affairs (2017). Chicago's Global Strategy: A model for effectively engaging the world. Chicago: Chicago Council on Global Affairs. Retrieved from https://www.thechicagocouncil.org/sites/default/files/report_chicagosglobalstrategy-170718.pdf

City Mayors Archive (n.d.) IULA promotes democratic local governments worldwide. Retrieved October 26, 2018, from http://www.citymayors.com/features/iula.html

City of Athens (n.d.) ACCMR - Athens Coordination Center. Retrieved July 26, 2018, from https://www.accmr.gr/en/the-athens-coordination-center.html

City of Melbourne (2008). *Business and International Committee Report: Melbourne Global Positioning Statement*. Retrieved from https://www.melbourne.vic.gov.au/about-council/committees-meetings/meeting-archive/MeetingAgendaItemAttachments/152/2502/BIRC_51_20080311.pdf

City of Melbourne (2014). *City of Melbourne Music Strategy: Supporting and Growing the City's Music Industry*. Retrieved from https://www.melbourne.vic.gov.au/SiteCollectionDocuments/music-strategy-final.pdf

City of Melbourne (2018a). About Melbourne. Retrieved from https://www.melbourne.vic.gov.au/about-melbourne/melbourne-profile/multicultural-communities/Pages/multicultural-communities.aspx

City of Melbourne (2018b). *Melbourne Music Plan 2018-21*. Retrieved from https://www.melbourne.vic.gov.au/SiteCollectionDocuments/melbourne-music-plan-2018.pdf

City of Zurich (2019). Integration Office. Retrieved July 9, 2019, from https://www.stadt-zuerich.ch/prd/en/index/stadtentwicklung/integrationsfoerderung.html

Clark, G. (2016). *Global Cities: A Short History*. Washington, D.C.: The Brookings Institution.

References

Coffey, H. (2017). Amsterdam has a new solution for overtourism. Retrieved October 18, 2018, from https://www.independent.co.uk/travel/news-and-advice/amsterdam-overtourism-solution-tourists-technology-van-gogh-museum-canal-boat-rides-a8015811.html

Confédération suisse (2019). *The 43 organizations and secretariats in Switzerland*. Retrieved from https://www.dfae.admin.ch/dam/mission-onu-omc-aele-geneve/en/documents/Tableau-des-OI_EN.pdf

Congostrina, A. (2018). Airbnb compartirà dades amb l'Ajuntament per caçar els pisos il·legals. *El País*.

Coombs, C. L. (2012). Cities and Political Prowess. *Diplomatic Courier*. Retrieved from https://www.diplomaticourier.com/posts/cities-and-political-prowess

Culture 21, UCLG, and Ciudad de México (2009). SAHA-GU: Gamcheon Culture Village Project.

DANE (2017). *Boletín técnico: Pobreza Monetaria Bogotá D.C. Año 2017*. Bogotá.

Eurocities (2016). *Social Affairs: Refugee Reception and Integration in Cities*. Retrieved from https://ec.europa.eu/futurium/sites/futurium/files/eurocities-refugees-report.pdf

Eurocities (2017). *Cities' Actions for the Education of Refugees and Asylum Seekers*. Retrieved from http://nws.eurocities.eu/MediaShell/media/Education report_Final Version.pdf

Eurocities (2018). Integrating Cities - Cities-Grow (2017-2019). Retrieved July 26, 2018, from http://www.integratingcities.eu/integrating-cities/projects/cities-grow

Euromonitor International (2017a). Passport Database - Cities.

Euromonitor International (2017b). *Top 100 City Destinations Ranking WTM London 2017 Edition*. Retrieved from http://go.euromonitor.com/rs/805-KOK-719/images/Euromonitor International_WTM London 2017_Top 100 City Destinations.pdf

Euronews (2017). Tourists flock back to Paris a year after terror attacks. Retrieved August 6, 2019, from https://www.euronews.com/2017/08/22/tourists-flock-back-to-paris-a-year-after-terror-attacks

fDi Intelligence - Financial Times (2019). Global Cities of the Future 2018/19.

Florida (2017). *The New Urban Crisis: how our cities are increasing inequality, deeping segregation, and failing the middle class - and what we can do about it*. New York: Basic Books.

Florida Chamber of Commerce (2017). *Florida Foreign Direct Investment Report*. Retrieved from www.FloridaChamber.com

Florida, R. (2014). Why Big Cities Matter in the Developing World. Retrieved October 5, 2018, from https://www.citylab.com/life/2014/01/why-big-cities-matter-developing-world/6025/

Friedmann, J. (1986). The World City Hypothesis. *Development and Change*, 17(1), 69–83.

GaWC (2018a). GaWC - The World According to GaWC. Retrieved November 16, 2018, from https://www.lboro.ac.uk/gawc/gawcworlds.html

GaWC (2018b). GaWC City Link Classification 2018. Retrieved July 17, 2019, from https://www.lboro.ac.uk/gawc/world2018link.html

Ghemawat, P., and Altman, S. A. (2016). DHL Global Connectedness Index 2016 -The State of Globalization in an Age of Ambiguity. Bonn: Deutsche Post DHL Group.

GOBankingRates (2018). These 19 Metro Areas Have the Biggest Wealth Gaps, Study Finds. Retrieved November 19, 2018, from https://www.gobankingrates.com/making-money/economy/cities-with-biggest-wealth-gaps/

Goodwin, H. (2017). *The Challenge of Overtourism* (Responsible Tourism Partnership Working Paper 4).

Gordon, D. J., and Johnson, C. A. (2018). City-networks, global climate governance, and the road to 1.5 °C. *Current Opinion in Environmental Sustainability*, 30, 35–41.

Guangzhou International Award for Urban Innovation. (2018). Busan, Republic of Korea - Gamcheon Culture Village's City Rejuvenation Project. Retrieved January 9, 2019, from http://www.guangzhouaward.org/award_d.aspx?CateId=289&newsid=1390

Haar, J. (2008). *International Trade Promotion Among Major American Cities: A study report prepared for the Jay Malina International Trade Consortium Miami-Dade County*.

Hall, P. (2005). The World's Urban Systems: A European Perspective. Retrieved January 19, 2018, from http://www.globalurban.org/Issue1PIMag05/Hall article.htm

Hamburg Marketing GmbH (n.d.) Hamburg Marketing. Retrieved January 15, 2019, from https://marketing.hamburg.de/homepage.html

References

Hamburg Marketing GmbH (2011). Working together for Hamburg. *Phi Delta Kappan*.

HKTDC (2018). Guangzhou (Guangdong) City Information. Retrieved August 6, 2018, from http://china-trade-research.hktdc.com/business-news/article/Facts-and-Figures/Guangzhou-Guangdong-City-Information/ff/en/1/1X000000/1X09VTH4.htm

Hong, S.-G., and Lee, H.-M. (2015). Developing Gamcheon Cultural Village as a tourist destination through co-creation. *Service Business*, 9, 749–769.

Hornberger, K. (2011). Investment Promotion with Impact: The Case of Invest in Bogota. Retrieved from http://www.mitpressjournals.org/doi/10.1162/rest.89.1.30

ICCA (2019). Past favourite Paris achieves landslide victory with return to first place in ICCA city rankings. Retrieved from https://www.iccaworld.org/npps/story.cfm?nppage=935584

INSEAD (2019). *The Global Talent Competitiveness Index 2019 Entrepreneurial Talent and Global Competitiveness*. Fontainebleau, France.

Invest in Bogota (2016). Bogota: A Global Center for Business and a Great Place to Live. Retrieved from https://www.deik.org.tr/uploads/ff5bad892d23463b9363a747543a4c33.pdf

Invest In Bogota (2018). General facts and figures of Bogota. Retrieved February 14, 2019, from https://en.investinbogota.org/why-bogota/general-facts-and-figures-bogota

Invest In Bogotá (2018). Bogota, the Latin American capital that creates most jobs with new foreign direct investment. Retrieved February 12, 2019, from https://en.investinbogota.org/news/bogota-capital-latinoamericana-con-mas-empleos-por-IED

IOM (2015). *World Migration Report 2015*. Geneva: International Organization for Migration.

IPK International (2016). *ITB World Travel Trends Report 2015/2016*. Munich.

ITU (2017). ICT Facts and Figures 2017. Geneva: International Telecommunication Union.

Järvisalo, S. (2012). How to build successful city brands? Case Munich, Berlin and Hamburg - Thesis. Retrieved from https://www.theseus.fi/bitstream/handle/10024/47992/City brands.pdf?sequence=1

Keiner, M., and Kim, A. (2007). Transnational City Networks for Sustainability. *European Planning Studies*, 15(10), 1369–1395.

Langill, M. (2015). Impacts on Thailand's Tourism Industry after the 2004 Indian Ocean Tsunami. Retrieved August 6, 2019, from https://asialasalle2015.wordpress.com/2015/09/17/impacts-on-thailands-tourism-industry-after-2004-indian-ocean-tsunami/

London & Partners (n.d.) About London & Partners. Retrieved August 6, 2018, from http://www.londonandpartners.com/about-us

London & Partners (2017). *Annual Review 2016-2017*. Retrieved from http://files.londonandpartners.com/l-and-p/assets/annual_review_2016-17.pdf

Manyika, J., Lund, S., Bughin, J., Woetzel, J., Stamenov, K., and Dhingra, D. (2016). Digital Globalization: The New Era of Global Flows. McKinsey & Company. Retrieved from www.mckinsey.com/mgi.

Mastercard (2018). Mastercard's 2018 Global Destination Cities Index. Retrieved July 17, 2019, from https://newsroom.mastercard.com/press-releases/big-cities-big-business-bangkok-london-and-paris-lead-the-way-in-mastercards-2018-global-destination-cities-index/

Mercer (2019). Quality of Living City Ranking. Retrieved July 8, 2019, from https://mobilityexchange.mercer.com/Insights/quality-of-living-rankings

MIA (2019). Cargo Modernization Program - Miami International Airport. Retrieved January 16, 2019, from http://www.miami-airport.com/cargo_modernization.asp

Miami-Dade County (2009). *Miami-Dade County Facts*. Retrieved from www.miamidade.gov/planzone

Miami-Dade County (2018a). International Trade & Commerce. Retrieved November 16, 2018, from https://www.miamidade.gov/business/international-trade.asp

Miami-Dade County (2018b). PortMiami - Miami-Dade County. Retrieved November 19, 2018, from http://www.miamidade.gov/portmiami/

MMF (2018). *Global Power City Index 2018*. Tokyo. Retrieved from http://mori-m-foundation.or.jp/pdf/GPCI2018_summary.pdf

Moskow, M. H., Osborn, W. A., and Leff, S. (2012). Foreign Direct Investment: Globalizing Chicago's Economic Development Plans. Chicago: The Chicago Council on Global Affairs.

Müller, A. (2019). Bevölkerung im Kanton Zürich: Mehr als 1,5 Millionen Zürcher. Retrieved July 8, 2019, from https://www.nzz.ch/zuerich/bevoelkerung-im-kanton-zuerich-mehr-als-15-millionen-zuercher-ld.1458291

Municipality of Amsterdam (2018). Tourism in Amsterdam Metropolitan Area.

Music Victoria (n.d.) How to: Agent of Change. Retrieved October 16, 2018, from https://www.musicvictoria.com.au/resources/agent-of-change-explained

Nguyen, D.-Q. (2017). Defining the 25% foreign population in Switzerland. Retrieved July 8, 2019, from https://www.swissinfo.ch/eng/migration-series-part-1-_who-are-the-25-foreign-population-in-switzerland/42412156

Nye, J. (2017). Soft power: the origins and political progress of a concept. *Palgrave Communications*, 3:17008.

Oguztimur, S., and Akturan, U. (2016). Synthesis of City Branding Literature (1988–2014) as a Research Domain. *International Journal OfTourism Research*, *18*, 357–372.

Open Data Network (2018). Gross Domestic Product. Retrieved July 26, 2018, from https://www.opendatanetwork.com/entity/310M200US12020/Athens_Metro_Area_GA/economy.gdp.per_capita_gdp?year=2016

Reputation Institute (2017). *2017 City RepTrak® The Most Reputable Cities in the World*. Retrieved from https://cdn2.hubspot.net/hubfs/2963875/Resources/2017-City-RepTrak-Report.pdf?submissionGuid=e1bed37e-065d-433d-b1b9-059fbcce6bd1

Reputation Institute (2018). *2018 City RepTrak - The World's Most Reputable Cities*. Retrieved from https://www.reputationinstitute.com/sites/default/files/pdfs/2018-City-RepTrak.pdf

Responsible Travel (n.d.) Overtourism in Venice. Retrieved October 18, 2018, from https://www.responsibletravel.com/copy/overtourism-in-venice

Rivenburgh, N. K. (2010). *The Olympic Games, media, and the challenges of global image making: university lecture on the Olympics*. Barcelona: Centre d'Estudis Olímpics (UAB).

Roberts, K. (2016). 1,439 multinationals from 55 nations in South Florida, and there are at least 4 key reasons - WorldCity, Inc. Retrieved January 16, 2019, from https://www.worldcityweb.com/1439-multinationals-from-55-nations-in-south-florida-and-there-are-at-least-4-key-reasons

Saskia Sassen, Peter Taylor, Ben Derudder, Frank Witlox, Jonathan Rutherford, Michael Hoyler, ... Davina Jackson (n.d.) Connecting Cities: Networks. Retrieved from https://www.metropolis.org/sites/default/files/network_complete_0.pdf

Sassen, S. (1991). *The Global City: New York, London, Tokyo*. Princeton - New Jersey: Princeton University Press.

SGS Economics and Planning (2017). *Economic Performance of Australia's cities and regions*.

Sharecity (2017). Athens. Retrieved from http://sharecity.ie/wp-content/uploads/2017/02/Athens-final.pdf

SITUR (2016). Anuario 2016. Medellin (Colombia): Sistema de Indicadores Turísticos Medellín-Antioquia.

Solidarity Cities (2018). Solidarity Cities. Retrieved July 26, 2018, from https://solidaritycities.eu/about

Stadt Zürich (2019a). Arbeitslosenzahlen Mai 2019. Retrieved July 8, 2019, from https://www.stadt-zuerich.ch/prd/de/index/statistik/kontakt-medien/aktuell/neuigkeiten/2019/2019-06-11_Arbeitslosenzahlen-Mai-2019.html

Stadt Zürich (2019b). Economy and Employment. Retrieved July 9, 2019, from https://www.stadt-zuerich.ch/portal/en/index/portraet_der_stadt_zuerich/wirtschaftsraum_u_-foerderung.html

State of Victoria (2013). *Victoria's Regional Tourism Strategy 2013-2016*. Retrieved from https://corp.rdp.tourismnortheast.com.au/wp-content/uploads/sites/54/6588_victoria_-regional_tourism_strategy_2013-16_WEB-1.pdf

State of Victoria (2017). *Victorian Visitor Economy Strategy Action Plan 2016-2020*. Retrieved from www.economicdevelopment.vic.gov.au

Statista (2017). Miami metro area population 2010-2017. Retrieved November 19, 2018, from https://www.statista.com/statistics/815202/miami-metro-area-population/

Statista (2019). Growth of global air traffic passenger demand from 2006 to 2019. Retrieved July 17, 2019, from https://www.statista.com/statistics/193533/growth-of-global-air-traffic-passenger-demand/

Terrill, A., Hogart, D., Clement, A., and Francis, R. (n.d.) *The Mastering of a Music City: Key Elements, Effective Strategies and why it's worth pursuing*. Retrieved from https://www.ifpi.org/downloads/The-Mastering-of-a-Music-City.pdf

The City of Miami (2016). *Strategic Plan - Annual Update 2016*. Retrieved from http://www.miamigov.com/strategicPlanning/docs/strategicPlanning/Strat_Plan_Final_Version_3-16-17.pdf

The Economist Intelligence Unit (2018). *The Global Liveability Index 2018*.

The Place Brand Observer (2017). How Hamburg Moved from Traditional Destination Marketing to Strategic City Branding. Retrieved January 15, 2019, from https://

placebrandobserver.com/destination-marketing-city-branding-example-hamburg/

Top Universities (2019). QS World University Rankings 2019. Retrieved July 9, 2019, from https://www.topuniversities.com/university-rankings/world-university-rankings/2019

Tourism Research Australia (2018). International Visitor Survey Results.

Tourism Victoria (2015). *Value of Tourism to Melbourne 2013-2014*. Retrieved from https://www.ecotourism.org.au/assets/Resources-Hub-Ecotourism-Research/Melbourne-TSA-Summary-2013-14-010216.pdf

Traveller AU (2018). Amsterdam tourism crack down: City looks to curb tourist "fun rides" and boozy boat trips. Retrieved October 18, 2018, from http://www.traveller.com.au/amsterdam-tourism-crack-down-city-looks-to-curb-fun-rides-and-boozy-tourists-h105yy

UN-Habitat (2018). Press Release: Cities need to move faster to meet their 2030 SDG targets. Retrieved October 8, 2018, from https://unhabitat.org/press-release-cities-need-to-move-faster-to-meet-their-2030-sdg-targets/

UN (2001). *The World of Investment Promotion At A Glance: A Survey of Investment Promotion Practices*. New York and Geneva. Retrieved from www.unctad.org/asit.

UNWTO (n.d.) Definition | Sustainable Development of Tourism. Retrieved August 10, 2018, from http://sdt.unwto.org/content/about-us-5

UNWTO (1995). UNWTO technical manual: Collection of Tourism Expenditure Statistics.

UNWTO (2017a). Tourism Highlights 2017 Edition. Madrid: World Tourism Organization (UNWTO).

UNWTO (2017b). Why tourism? Retrieved August 1, 2018, from http://www2.unwto.org/content/why-tourism

UNWTO (2018). *UNWTO Annual Report 2017*. Madrid: World Tourism Organization (UNWTO). http://doi.org/10.18111/9789284419807

van der Pluijm, R. (2007). *City Diplomacy: The Expanding Role of Cities in International Politics*. The Hague. Retrieved from http://www.clingendael.nl

Venezia today (2018). Turismo in Veneto, crescita senza sosta: nel 2017 Venezia registra il +8% di arrivi. Retrieved October 18, 2018, from http://www.veneziatoday.it/cronaca/venezia-turismo-crescita-costante-2017.html

References

Victoria State Government (2017). *Economic Contribution of Tourism to Melbourne.* Retrieved from https://assets.destination.melbourne/resources/Melbourne-RTSA-2015-16-FINAL.pdf?mtime=20171106161846

Visit Victoria (2018). Melbourne Live Music Capital Of The World. Retrieved October 16, 2018, from https://corporate.visitvictoria.com/news/melbourne-live-music-capital-of-the-world

WEF (2017). *Migration and Its Impact on Cities.* Geneva: World Economic Forum.

World Shipping Council (n.d.) Top 50 World Container Ports. Retrieved January 7, 2019, from http://www.worldshipping.org/about-the-industry/global-trade/top-50-world-container-ports

WTTC (2018). Travel and Tourism Economic Impact 2018. London: World Travel & Tourism Council (WTTC). Retrieved from https://www.wttc.org/-/media/files/reports/economic-impact-research/regions-2018/world2018.pdf

Z/Yen, and CDI (2019). *The Global Financial Centres Index 25.* Retrieved from https://www.longfinance.net/media/documents/GFCI_25_Report.pdf

6. Appendix I: Additional Resources

On the IESE Cities in Motion Strategies website you will find additional related material and resources. Check the following links regularly to access our latest publications:

• IESE Cities in Motion Strategies: www.iese.edu/cim.

Additionally, the authors recommend the following Internet resources for more information on the topic:

• 100 Resilient Cities: www.100resilientcities.org.
• C40 (Cities Climate Leadership Groups): www.c40.org.
• Chicago Council on Global Affairs: www.thechicagocouncil.org.
• Cities Alliance: www.citiesalliance.org.
• Cities for Mobility: www.cities-for-mobility.net.
• Cities Programme: https://citiesprogramme.org.
• City Prosperity Initiative: http://cpi.unhabitat.org.
• Climate Alliance: www.climatealliance.org
• Compact of Mayors: www.compactofmayors.org.
• EUROCITIES: www.eurocities.eu.
• Global Cities Business Alliance: www.businessincities.com.
• Habitat III – The New Urban Agenda: https://habitat3.org.
• ICLEI (Local Governments for Sustainability): www.iclei.org.
• Leading Cities: http://leadingcities.org.
• LSE Cities: https://lsecities.net.

Appendix I: Additional Resources

- MedCités: www.medcities.org.
- Metropolis: www.metropolis.org.
- Mori Memorial Foundation: http://mori-m-foundation.or.jp.
- New Cities Foundation: www.newcitiesfoundation.org.
- OECD: www.oecd.org.
- Open Cities: www.opencities.eu.
- PPPs for Cities: www.pppcities.org.
- Proyecto Al-las: www.proyectoallas.net.
- Sister Cities International: www.sistercities.org.
- Sustainable Development Knowledge Platform: https://sustainabledevelopment.un.org.
- The Global Task Force: www.global-taskforce.org.
- UN-Habitat: http://unhabitat.org.
- UN-Data: http://data.un.org.
- United Cities and Local Governments (UCLG): www.uclg.org.
- United Nations Statistics Division (UNstats): http://unstats.un.org.
- UN Sustainable Development Goals (SDGs): https://sustainabledevelopment.un.org.
- URBACT: http://urbact.eu.
- World Association of Investment Promotion Agencies (WAIPA): www.waipa.org.
- World Bank: www.worldbank.org.
- World Economic Forum: www.weforum.org.

7. Appendix II: CIM Index - International Outreach Dimension

This appendix includes a brief presentation of the IESE Cities in Motion Index, focusing on the international outreach dimension. For more information on the index, please check the IESE Cities in Motion website www.iese.edu/cim, with all our latest publications.

CITIES IN MOTION INDEX

The Cities in Motion Index (*CIMI*) has been designed with the aim of constructing a "breakthrough" indicator in terms of its completeness, characteristics, comparability and the quality and objectivity of its information. Its goal is to enable measurement of the future sustainability of the world's main cities, as well as the quality of life of their inhabitants.

The CIM model originally considers 10 key dimensions for a city: governance, urban planning, public management, technology, the environment, international outreach, social cohesion, mobility and transportation, human capital, and the economy. All the indicators are linked with a strategic aim that leads to a novel form of local economic development: the creation of a global city, the promotion of the entrepreneurial spirit, and innovation, among others.

However, as in the previous edition, the 2019 edition merges two of the abovementioned dimensions: governance and public management (in a dimension called simply "governance"). Therefore, the 2019 edition covers nine key dimensions for the years 2016, 2017 and 2018 and includes 174 cities — 79 of them capitals — representing 80 countries.

RANKING *CIMI* 2018

Year after year, the top place in the ranking seems to be disputed by London (United Kingdom) and New York (United States), two highly developed and smart cities. This year, London is in first place in the overall ranking, thanks to its performance in the dimensions of international outreach (position 1), human capital (position 1), mobility and transportation (position 3) and the economy (position 12). However, the city does not show such a good performance in the dimension of social cohesion (position 45).

New York is in second place in the overall ranking, thanks to its performance in the dimensions of the economy (position 1), human capital (position 3), urban planning (position 2) and mobility and transportation (position 5). As in previous years, it shows a worse performance in social cohesion (position 137) and the environment (position 78) and, although it has made some improvement in the latter with respect to the previous year, it has not achieved an outstanding position.

Lastly, the city of Amsterdam completes the podium. The capital of the Netherlands has improved a lot in international outreach (position 2), also standing out for the economy, urban planning, and mobility and transportation.

The 2019 CIMI exhibits a dominance of European cities in the top positions of the ranking, with seven Western European cities in the top 10 positions (see Table A1). Moreover, of the top 50 positions in the overall ranking, more than half are occupied by European cities. Additionally, 13 of them are located in North America, five in Asia and four in Oceania.

Appendix II: CIM Index - International Outreach Dimension

TABLE A1. CITY RANKING. TOP 10

CIMI 2015	City (Country)
1	London - United Kingdom
2	New York - USA
3	Amsterdam - Netherlands
4	Paris - France
5	Reykjavík - Iceland
6	Tokyo - Japan
7	Singapore - Singapore
8	Copenhagen - Denmark
9	Berlin - Germany
10	Vienna - Austria

DIMENSION: INTERNATIONAL OUTREACH

Cities that want to progress must secure a privileged place in the world. Maintaining global impact involves improving the city brand and its international recognition through strategic tourism plans, the attracting of foreign investment and representation abroad.

Cities can have a greater or lesser international outreach even if they are from the same country, but this is not independent of the degree of openness nationally. This dimension seeks to reflect these differences and to measure the international outreach of cities.

In this respect, the following indicators have been included: number of passengers by airport, number of McDonald's restaurants per city, the restaurant index, the number of hotels per capita, ranking of the most popular places in the world according to Sightsmap, and the number of meetings and conferences that are held according to data from the ICCA. Table A2 summarizes these indicators, along with descriptions of them, their units of measurement, and the source of the information. All indicators of this dimension, except Sightsmap, are incorporated with a positive sign into the calculation of the CIMI since the higher the value of the indicators, the greater the impact that the city has on the world.

TABLE A2. INTERNATIONAL OUTREACH INDICATORS

Indicator	Description / Unit of measurement	Source
McDonald's	Number of McDonald's restaurants per city.	OpenStreetMap
Number of passengers per airport	Number of passengers per airport in thousands.	Euromonitor
Sightsmap	Ranking of cities according to the number of photos taken in the city and uploaded to Panoramio (community for sharing photographs online). The top positions correspond to the cities with the most photographs.	Sightsmap
Number of conferences and meetings	Number of international conferences and meetings that take place in a city.	International Congress and Convention Association (ICCA)
Hotels	Number of hotels per capita.	OpenStreetMap
Restaurant index	The index shows the prices of food and beverages in restaurants and bars compared to New York City.	Numbeo

RANKING – INTERNATIONAL OUTREACH DIMENSION

London (United Kingdom) leads this dimension, while Amsterdam (Netherlands) and Paris (France) are in second and third place, respectively. London is among the cities with the highest number of airline passengers, something consistent with it having the largest number of air routes, and it also stands out for the significant number of hotels it has and the amount of international conferences that it organizes. Amsterdam stands out, just like the British capital, for the number of airline passengers and the large number of international conferences. The French capital, for its part, is in third place in the international outreach ranking with the most photographs uploaded to Panoramio and comes second for the organization of international meetings and congresses, as well as for having a large number of hotels. Of the top 10 cities for this dimension, five are European, two are North American and two are from Oceania.

TABLE A3. RANKING BY DIMENSION: INTERNATIONAL OUTREACH

City-Country	International Outreach	Cities in Motion 2018
London - United Kingdom	1	1
Amsterdam - Netherlands	2	3
Paris - France	3	4
Singapore - Singapore	4	7
Berlin - Germany	5	9
Melbourne - Australia	6	20
Vienna - Austria	7	10
New York - USA	8	2
Miami - USA	9	40
Sydney - Australia	10	19
Barcelona - Spain	11	28
Palma de Mallorca - Spain	12	88
Geneva - Switzerland	13	32
Rome - Italy	14	75
Hong Kong - China	15	11
Copenhagen - Denmark	16	8
Madrid - Spain	17	24
Chicago - USA	18	17
Oslo - Norway	19	14
Prague - Czech Republic	20	47
Zurich - Switzerland	21	15

Appendix II: CIM Index - International Outreach Dimension

City-Country	International Outreach	Cities in Motion 2018
Reykjavík - Iceland	22	5
Bangkok - Thailand	23	104
Stockholm - Sweden	24	13
Dubai - United Arab Emirates	25	99
Lisbon - Portugal	26	44
Toronto - Canada	27	18
Munich - Germany	28	27
Buenos Aires - Argentina	29	77
Dublin - Ireland	30	37
Milan - Italy	31	41
Frankfurt - Germany	32	33
Los Angeles - USA	33	16
Seoul - South Korea	34	12
Tokyo - Japan	35	6
San Francisco - USA	36	21
Budapest - Hungary	37	73
Edinburgh - United Kingdom	38	46
Helsinki - Finland	39	22
Washington - USA	40	23
Montreal - Canada	41	38
Nice - France	42	85
Phoenix - USA	43	42
Denver - USA	44	52
Brussels - Belgium	45	48
Hamburg - Germany	46	34
Düsseldorf - Germany	47	50
Istanbul - Turkey	48	118
Basel - Switzerland	49	29
Beijing - China	50	83

Appendix II: CIM Index - International Outreach Dimension

City-Country	International Outreach	Cities in Motion 2018
Auckland - New Zealand	51	35
San Diego - USA	52	49
Warsaw - Poland	53	69
Abu Dhabi - United Arab Emirates	54	127
Taipei - Taiwan	55	30
Houston - USA	56	60
Santiago - Chile	57	66
Vancouver - Canada	58	55
Shanghai - China	59	59
Glasgow - United Kingdom	60	64
Athens - Greece	61	106
Málaga - Spain	62	80
Cologne - Germany	63	51
Kuala Lumpur - Malaysia	64	100
Jerusalem - Israel	65	123
Duisburg - Germany	66	90
Seattle - USA	67	58
Florence - Italy	68	108
Boston - USA	69	25
São Paulo - Brazil	70	132
Mexico City - Mexico	71	133
Rio de Janeiro - Brazil	72	128
Moscow - Russia	73	86
Manchester - United Kingdom	74	78
Lyon - France	75	56
Bogotá - Colombia	76	117
Saint Petersburg - Russia	77	121
Bucharest - Romania	78	103
Wellington - New Zealand	79	26

Appendix II: CIM Index - International Outreach Dimension

City-Country	International Outreach	Cities in Motion 2018
Birmingham - United Kingdom	80	63
Panama - Panama	81	114
New Delhi - India	82	166
Göteborg - Sweden	83	36
Doha - Qatar	84	126
Dallas - USA	85	45
Porto - Portugal	86	91
Marseille - France	87	89
Philadelphia - USA	88	54
Stuttgart - Germany	89	53
Guangzhou - China	90	113
Baltimore - USA	91	71
Rotterdam - Netherlands	92	43
Riga - Latvia	93	84
Ho Chi Minh City - Vietnam	94	122
Tallinn - Estonia	95	65
Belgrade - Serbia	96	120
Seville - Spain	97	76
Ottawa - Canada	98	39
Eindhoven - Netherlands	99	57
San José - Costa Rica	100	112
Turin - Italy	101	109
Jakarta - Indonesia	102	142
San Antonio - USA	103	62
Tel Aviv - Israel	104	81
Manila - Philippines	105	163
Bangalore - India	106	153
Valencia - Spain	107	61
Vilnius - Lithuania	108	74

Appendix II: CIM Index - International Outreach Dimension

City-Country	International Outreach	Cities in Motion 2018
Cape Town - South Africa	109	158
Montevideo - Uruguay	110	92
Naples - Italy	111	116
Bern - Switzerland	112	31
Osaka - Japan	113	68
Quebec - Canada	114	67
Sofia - Bulgaria	115	115
Quito - Ecuador	116	137
Kuwait City - Kuwait	117	143
Brasília - Brazil	118	130
Manama - Bahrain	119	159
La Paz - Bolivia	120	145
Mumbai - India	121	161
Bratislava - Slovakia	122	70
Kiev - Ukraine	123	111
Caracas - Venezuela	124	172
Bilbao - Spain	125	107
Shenzhen - China	126	119
Liverpool - United Kingdom	127	94
Leeds - United Kingdom	128	79
Antwerp - Belgium	129	72
Zagreb - Croatia	130	97
Nagoya - Japan	131	82
Tbilisi - Georgia	132	124
Santo Domingo - Dominican Republic	133	139
Ljubljana - Slovenia	134	93
Wroclaw - Poland	135	95
Lima - Peru	136	138

Appendix II: CIM Index - International Outreach Dimension

City-Country	International Outreach	Cities in Motion 2018
Lille - France	137	98
Rosario - Argentina	138	125
Salvador - Brazil	139	146
Santa Cruz - Bolivia	140	147
Amman - Jordan	141	150
Ankara - Turkey	142	135
Baku - Azerbaijan	143	131
Guatemala City - Guatemala	144	160
Nairobi - Kenya	145	162
Minsk - Belarus	146	110
Nottingham - United Kingdom	147	96
Córdoba - Argentina	148	136
Zaragoza - Spain	149	101
A Coruña - Spain	150	102
Casablanca - Morocco	151	155
Curitiba - Brazil	152	140
Linz - Austria	153	87
Skopje - North Macedonia	154	149
Medellín - Colombia	155	134
Guayaquil - Ecuador	156	152
Riyadh - Saudi Arabia	157	164
Sarajevo - Bosnia-Herzegovina	158	144
Cairo - Egypt	159	165
Belo Horizonte - Brazil	160	151
Tianjin - China	161	154
Asunción - Paraguay	162	141
Murcia - Spain	163	105
Johannesburg - South Africa	164	167
Novosibirsk - Russia	165	156

Appendix II: CIM Index - International Outreach Dimension

City-Country	International Outreach	Cities in Motion 2018
Lahore - Pakistan	166	173
Almaty - Kazakhstan	167	129
Tunis - Tunisia	168	157
Rabat - Morocco	169	168
Cali - Colombia	170	148
Kolkata - India	171	169
Douala - Cameroon	172	170
Lagos - Nigeria	173	171
Karachi - Pakistan	174	174

Printed in Great Britain
by Amazon